SPECIAL EFFECTS IN
BOBBIN
Lace

SPECIAL EFFECTS IN
BOBBIN *Lace*

Over 20 patterns using colour in bobbin lace

SANDI WOODS

B.T. BATSFORD LTD, LONDON

Dedication
To The U.M.

ACKNOWLEDGEMENTS

I would like to thank my husband, Phil Woods, and my daughters,
Melissa and Bethany, for their help, support and understanding, especially
when meals have not appeared to be forthcoming. In particular, I have valued
the expertise and encouragement of Patricia Read who, with Lucy Kincaid,
researched the Milanese braids and produced them with such clarity
in their books, *Milanese Lace* and *New Braids and Designs in Milanese Lace*.
I am also grateful to them for allowing me to use the braids in this book.
Special thanks to the Swanley Lacemakers and all other lacemakers
for their interest and willingness to test the patterns, to Barry Adams
for the loan of 'B', and to Christine and David Springett for their notes on magic threads.

First published in 1998 by
B.T. Batsford Ltd
583 Fulham Road
London SW6 5BY

A catalogue record for this book is available from the British Library.

ISBN 0 7134 8071 8

Printed in Singapore

Photography by Sandi Woods

CONTENTS

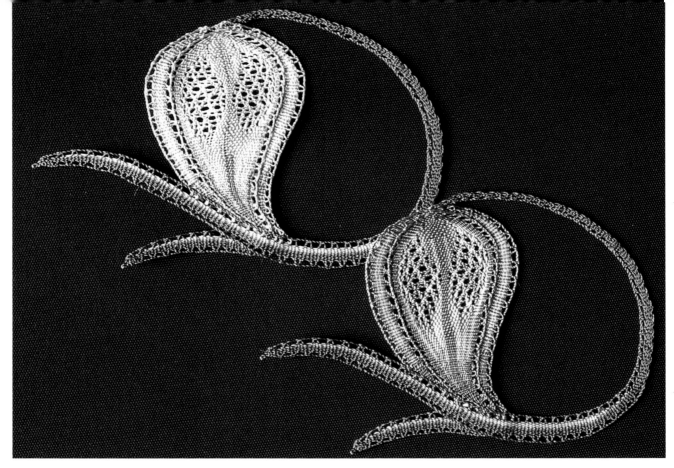

Crocus. Version 2 (left), version 1 (right). Pipers Silks 80/3 and 90/3

ABBREVIATIONS

½ st	half st
Cls	cloth (or whole) st
Cls & Tw	cloth/st & Tw
cont	continue
diag, diags	diagram, diagrams
edge st	no (colour) change edge st, X T T X T T
foll	following
incl	inclusive
L	left
MTh	magic thread
no, nos	number, numbers
patt	pattern
pr, prs	pair, pairs
rem	remaining
rep	repeat
R	right

st	stitch
temp pin	temporary pin (indicated in the diagrams by a small circle, sometimes with a line from it)
thro	through
T O & T B	tie off & throw back
tog	together
T.S.	turning stitch, X T X T X (indicated on the diagrams by a circle, O)
Tw	twist (indicated on the diagrams by a small dash, e.g. 1 dash = 1 twist ╱, 2 dashes = 2 twists ╫)
var	variation
X T	cross - turn (½ st)
X T X	cross - turn - cross (Cls)
X T X T X	cross - turn - cross - turn - cross (turning st)
X T T X T T	cross - turn - turn - cross - turn - turn (no colour change edge st)

INTRODUCTION

Adopting a painterly use of colour in lacemaking is no more unusual than an artist choosing to work with colour. In many ways the same principles apply.

When painting, an artist chooses the colours with a particular use in mind. In making this choice, many factors will be considered, and the priorities for making a choice in one instance will almost certainly be changed in the next.

If the work is figurative, one of the broad priorities will be to choose colours which will describe the form of the subject. The starting point for making this colour choice will probably be to use its local colour, e.g. the leaf is green. If the leaf is painted in flat colour without added tones and shading, the result will be very different from a leaf where many shades, tones, highlights and reflected light are used. One end result will not necessarily be better than another, but if the completed work does not convey the artist's intentions then the point of creating the work is lost.

Another prime consideration could be the emotional use of colour to convey a sense of time and mood which can add to the narrative aspect of the work. If the example of a leaf is taken again, a sharply bright green leaf would normally be suggestive of springlike qualities, whereas the same leaf depicted in oranges and browns would suggest autumn. This is an obvious example to use, but if it is taken further with the additional consideration of a light source, then there are even more opportunities to develop the relevant narrative theme. If the same springlike leaf has warmer yellows added where highlights need to be placed, then depending upon the type of yellow and the depth and colour of the shadows, it could be suggesting sunset or a summer afternoon. Alternatively, the autmnal leaf could be given warm highlights to suggest a warm autumnal day, or if white was added to its edges, then frost and a cold day would be suggested.

Whenever a colour is added to the work, it has an immediate effect on everything else already worked. No colour is ever seen in isolation, nor can it be added without affecting the way in which all other colours are perceived. Colours can be added to the work to provide a compositional link that will direct the way in which the work is viewed and build up relationships with existing colours.

When an artist paints, as each colour is applied, the function that the colour is to perform will be considered and its relationship with existing colours evaluated. Colours can be changed, mixed, over-glazed or altered in many ways. The painting is built up gradually with constant adjustments.

In the same way, a lacemaker can place threads alongside one another and allow the eye to mix the colours visually. If an exact colour is unobtainable, then the available colour can be influenced by placing another beside it. If the work has not progressed too far, it may be possible to undo, or take out, whole sections if the colour is unsatisfactory. However, to prevent damage to threads and time being wasted, it really is essential to make a colour study before work commences.

In making a colour study, virtually all the main colour decisions are made, and problems can be resolved before work on the pillow starts. Technical details can also be planned and the manipulation of threads plotted. It is worth remembering that the colours of the threads and their relationships will appear very different once they are on the pricking card.

It is not usually possible to build up the colours of the work in the same way that the artist does when painting, because the order of work is dictated by the techniques employed: e.g. if top sewings or rolled work are to be a feature, then those sections which will appear to the fore when the work is finished must be worked first.

When making the colour study, the colours used will relate to themselves; they form visual colour notes only. When the threads for the lace are chosen they can never appear to match exactly those used for the study since they are of a different medium. The colours of the threads will form their own balance and relative values. Coloured pencils worked on tracing paper or layout paper provide one of the simplest and most effective ways to create a colour study. This study can then be placed over a pricking to establish exact positions of colour reference.

One of the major considerations when working with colour is the choice of thread. As with any other lace project, much depends on the type of lace to be worked. Texture is just as important as with monochromatic lace and can greatly alter the character of the work. However, the overriding issue is the colour range and its continuing availability.

It is worth noting that the larger manufacturers are often market led, and the market which leads may be the fashion industry, rather than lacemaking or other crafts which are comparatively small users. It is worth making a choice and building up a selection of colours from a range rather in the way an artist does with tubes of paint. It is less economic to buy only the specific threads for each project, since quantity cannot be accurately assessed. Although several threads in this book have been suggested, the patterns have been designed as a series and it will be found that the basic palette of colours in the earlier pieces is extended as the book progresses.

Cotton is available in a reasonable range of colours and is certainly strong enough to use. However, if the design contains tight bends, there is a tendency for the thread to buckle if it is tightly packed. Silk is available in a wide range of colours and has the added advantage of being reflective. Depending upon whether the silk is spun, with a soft sheen, or twisted gloss with obviously much higher reflective properties, the need for exact colour shades can be affected. A gloss silk thread will reflect and therefore blend more closely with its neighbour than a cotton thread can. Silk, particularly gloss silk, is extremely strong and has the advantage that it will compress very firmly without buckling when worked tightly around bends.

This book seeks to help the reasonably experienced lacemaker, competent in basic lacemaking techniques though not neccessarily possessing a high level of skill, who would like to use colour in a painterly way but perhaps is daunted by envisaged problems. The patterns do not specifically become more difficult in sequence as the book progresses. It is simply that more possibilities are explored and additional and alternative techniques are used, though it would be a confident lacemaker indeed who made a start with Sea Swirl or On Reflection.

Chapter 1, Getting Started with Colour, is designed to give an opportunity to the lacemaker to see the movement of the threads and the effects achieved without making any colour decisions. The patterns included are essentially sample pieces. The instructions are totally comprehensive and allow the lacemaker to practise and build upon techniques learned, using comparatively few colours. In Chapter 2, Painting with Threads, there are still designs that offer completely detailed instructions, but the emphasis at the end of the chapter is for the lacemaker to have a greater personal input and create an original interpretation of the designs. All of the designs in the earlier part of this chapter contain elements that are found in Sea Swirl and On Reflection. Chapter 3, Explaining Ideas, contains work that predates Sea Swirl and On Reflection, but the designs are included owing to the employment of some techniques that would not otherwise be covered by this book.

Hopefully this book will offer a few short cuts to lacemakers already using colour adventurously, and provide encouragement and help to those who would like to. There are no set rules to follow but sometimes understanding how an effect has been achieved can help to narrow down the potential for disaster.

All of the designs in this book can be worked monochromatically, in which case it will be preferable to use traditional techniques. The techniques devised for working in a painterly way deceive the eye because of the way colour is perceived; they are not recommended if, perhaps, the designs are worked in white.

HINTS ON WORKING

BEFORE STARTING
- Enlarge working diagram.
- Make colour study if not following suggested colour scheme.
- Copy pricking to draw a plan of leaders' working route.
- Ensure that where possible the leaders work at a 90-degree angle to the passive threads, unless a special effect is required, e.g. to emphasize perspective.
- Plan the most appropriate position for any blind pins.
- Scratch guidelines on to the pricking card to indicate design changes in colour, e.g. adding shadows.

- If a section of work has many pin references and different techniques happening almost simultaneously, place pins (preferably short, but not berry pins) into the marked holes and push right down, to serve as reminders.

WORKING

- As when working Milanese lace, bobbins need to be of similar weight and, to allow for making numerous sewings, the spangles should not be too large.
- To avoid wasting thread when working in colour, it is advisable to wind one bobbin of each pair fully, then pull out a smaller estimated amount to wind on to the other bobbin for each section.
- Tension pairs before and after working edge stitch.
- To achieve a smooth blending of colours, add pairs or threads placed singly, alternating with existing threads.
- When adding pairs to become part of a given listed order, add pairs forming the correct sequence from the outer edges first.
- Changing the tonal value or colour of the leaders can sometimes save changing several passive pairs when altering the colour of a braid.
- When adding pairs on temporary pins, lower the new pairs gently, using a pin to guide them into position.
- Adding passive pairs in a relevant colour to a braid pattern will emphasize design line or can be used to indicate shadows, e.g. a dark blue pair is worked along the inside edge of Lotus 1, section 2 (and other sections) of On Reflection.

- To achieve an even tension when working Tenstick, do not try to work too fast, and tension threads: (a) before working the pinned edge stitch, hold smooth edge pair to prevent movement; (b) after working first passive pair past pin; (c) after working X T X T at smooth edge, then work final X to complete stitch and place edge pair carefully at 90-degree angle to the work.
- Support pins can be used, especially when working a wide section of Tenstick or to stop a turning stitch slipping.
- To avoid confusion when working the scroll or a scroll method, push all other pins right down. As the scroll is worked, leave the pins standing as an aid to counting the pairs that have already been used. Alternatively, after numbering the pairs to be used for the scroll (see 1.10), place a marker pin or divider in front of the next passive pair to be worked to the outer edge. This will separate the pairs that have been worked from the pairs yet to be worked.
- Take care that the passive threads are not caught up around the scroll centre pin.
- Rolled scroll: add the extra pairs, in the required colours for rolling, to be temporarily worked as passives next to the inside edge pair, e.g. if 4 pairs are to be used for the start of the roll, add 4 pairs when setting up for scroll. Take care not to include them in the scroll method.
- When leaving a section of work for any length of time, make a locking stitch.

- Use magic threads to facilitate making sewings.
- When making sewings, where there are two colours in the pair, choose the most appropriate colour to make the loop.
- When joining one braid to another, if many sewings will be made into one pinhole, or if the threads will show too obtrusively on the right side of the work (due to their contrasting colours), work a twisted bar in a sympathetic colour, and make the sewings into the bar.

FINISHING WORK

- When working with colour, do not cut off threads too soon; they may be needed later.
- When tying off threads, especially when working with silk, do not just throw pairs back. Always tie 1½ reef knots to secure threads, even in cloth stitch.
- Do not cut the ends of threads too short while still working the piece, as working and moving a cover cloth over the ends could cause them to unravel, especially if they are of silk. The ends may be trimmed more closely when work is completely finished.
- Do not leave the ends of the threads too long or they will simply hinder the work in progress.
- When finishing at a point, tie off and throw back the remaining threads in a bunch and secure to work with pairs previously tied off.

Note: When working some of the braids it will be necessary to refer to *Milanese Lace* and *New Designs and Braids* in *Milanese Lace* (see Further Reading, page 126).

GETTING STARTED WITH COLOUR

Chapter 1

This series of patterns has been planned to illustrate the painterly use of colour and design while using traditional skills and techniques, each subsequent pattern building upon ideas previously explored. When working coloured lace in a painterly way, the wholly traditional techniques will not always be suitable to achieve the desired effects, hence the need in these sample pieces for step-by-step instructions showing the actual manipulation of the individual coloured threads.

Each of the four Afternoon Dainty motifs is slightly different, and for variety the instructions are given in four different colourways, predominantly blue, red, green and yellow. The green version incorporates just four different shades of thread, whereas the other three each incorporate nine. The shades of thread have been carefully chosen so that they provide a useful basis for building up a palette of related colours.

The two following motifs, Second Thoughts and Afterthoughts, may each be worked in any of the four colourways, although the detailed instructions are given in blue. Morning Glory and Budding Glory are motifs that can only be worked in blue or red using the instructions given.

When working the motifs, you will notice that the darker tones of the main flower colours have been used in the stem sections. This is to add coherence to the design and achieve a richness of colour in the darker tones, the exception being in version 4, where the same principle applies but the effect is achieved in a slightly different way.

It is possible to work the motifs in a variety of threads (see chart 1.1). Note that the pricking size given may have to be altered to accommodate the differing thickness of threads.

Right: Afternoon Dainties. Clockwise from top: version 1, version 2, version 4 and version 3. Pipers Silks 80/3 and 90/3

1.1 Thread comparison chart for Chapter 1

Colours	Abb	Pipers	G'mann	Colcot	Mad
Medium Green	MG	Dark Green 80/3	585	5053	713
Dark Green	DG	Bottle 90/3	237	5034	780
V Dark Green	VDG	Dk Tartan 80/3	472	5018	790
White	W	White 300	800	7001	501
Cream	C	White 300	802	6018	752
Dark Cream	DC	Ecru 80/3	5	6018	504
Light Blue	LB	Sky 90/3	143	4060	745
Medium Blue	MB	Delft 90/3	213	4053	580
Dark Blue: Purple	DB:Pp	Helio 90/3	218	4039	583
V Dark Blue	VDB	Navy 80/3	309	4005	630
Purple	Pp	Purple 80/3	810	4024	645
Light Pink	LP	Blush 90/3	659	3009	590
Dark Pink	DP	Strawberry 90/3	890	3014	592
Fuschia	F	Cranberry 80/3	384	3007	595
V Dark Red	VDR	Maroon 80/3	130	3005	787
Lt Straw Yellow	LY	Cream 80/3	325	1002	738
Dk Straw Yellow	DY	Butter 90/3	893	5040	610
Light Flesh Pink	LFP	Flesh 80/3	658	3011	740
Dark Flesh Pink	DFP	Rose 90/3	889	3010	591
Olive Green	OG	Apple Grn 80/3	582	5056	775

Notes

Pipers Silks 80/3, 90/3 and 300 Semi-gloss threads are
   interchangeable.

G'mann = Gutermann Silk S 303 or Polyester Sew All threads.

Colcot = Colcoton Unikat 34/2 or 70/2 threads.

Mad = Madeira Tanne 30 or 50, also known as Cotona threads.

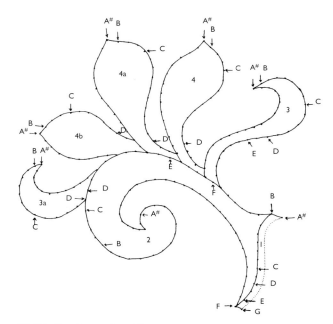

Thread	Pricking size
Pipers Silks 80/3, 90/3 and 300 Semi-gloss	100%
Gutermann Silks S 303	100%
Madeira Tanne 50	100%
Gutermann Polyester Sew All	95%
Colcoton Unikat 70/2	105%
Madeira Tanne 30	105%
Colcoton Unikat 34/2	110%

*1.3 Right: Pin reference plan – Afternoon Dainties,
versions 1–4 stem and petals, versions 1 & 4 leaves*

AFTERNOON DAINTIES

Pricking Size: See 1.2a versions 1 & 4, see 1.2b versions 2 & 3

100%: Pipers Silks:

80/3 Spun silk

90/3 Gloss silk

Semi-gloss 300

Gutermann Silk S303

Madeira Tanne 50

95%: Gutermann Polyester Sew-All

105%: Madeira Tanne 30

Colcoton Unikat 70/2

110%: Colcoton Unikat 34/2

Thread: See thread chart 1.1 for colour abbreviations and specific thread types. Do not mix different threads while working one motif, except when using Pipers Silks, where 80/3 and 90/3 are interchangeable. Likewise, Semi-gloss 300 White or 90/3 White may be used, but again do not mix them in the same motif.

AFTERNOON DAINTY, VERSION 1

Colours: Med Green MG

Dark Green DG

V Dark Green VDG

White W

Light Blue LB

Med Blue MB

Dark Blue:Purple DB:Pp

V Dark Blue VDB

Purple Pp

Techniques: No (colour) change edge stitch

Tenstick colour start

Mixing thread colours

Blind pin

Scroll (colour)

Changing leaders with passive pr

Turning stitch

Top sewings

One-colour point start

False picot

Rearranging threads

Changing colour of leaders

Stitches and Braids: Tenstick

Cloth stitch

Maltese spot

Lattice 1

Orchid 1

To Work: Work each section numerically as shown in 1.3. No (colour) change edge st and top sewings are used throughout. Colours /threads are shown singly in thread order listings, unless shown otherwise.

1.2a Prickings – Afternoon Dainties, versions 1 & 4

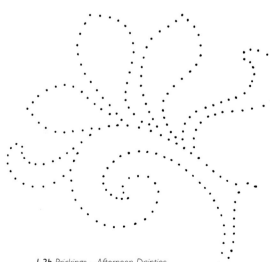

1.2b Prickings – Afternoon Dainties, versions 2 & 3

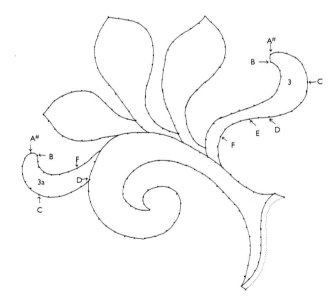

1.4 Pin reference plan – Afternoon Dainties, versions 2 & 3 leaves

SECTION 1, STEM

Note: Check that pin A# is correctly indentified.

*START at pin A#:

Hang 3 prs on pin in order VDB

DG

VDB (see 1.5)

Cls (X T X) inner pr VDB thro pr DG

Tw 2 pr DG

X T X T X both prs VDB tog

Now, leaders are pr VDB and pinned edge pr is DG

Hang on temp pins (see 1.6) 3 prs VDG

1 pr VDB

alternating threads as shown, and twisting the two central passive threads tog (7 prs)

Cls leaders VDB thro passive prs to pin B

Work the no (colour) change edge st as foll:

Tw 2 leaders, pin B under leaders

X T T X T T with pinned edge pr

Note: The pinned edge pr and the leaders have not changed.

Cont in Tenstick, working X T X T X at the smooth edge

After pin C has been worked:

T O & T B 1pr VDG, single passives 2 & 3 (from pinned edge)

After pin D:

T O & T B 1pr VDG/VDB, single passives 2 & 3

After pin E:

T O & T B 1pr VDG/VDB, single passives 2 & 3 (4 prs)

Note: Do not cut off prs thrown back; they will be needed later to secure threads.

After pin F:

Cls leaders VDB thro 1st passive pr VDG

T O & T B leaders, pr VDB

Using pin G as a support (place pin after X T):

Cls outer edge pr VDB thro rem passive pr VDG

T O pr VDB

T O pr VDG, do not throw these prs back yet

Untwist pinned edge pr DG, use it to tie prs VDB & VDG in a bunch

T B 3 prs DG, VDB & VDG (tied in bunch) and use the previously T O & T B prs, from pins E & D, to secure to work

*

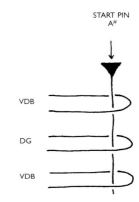

1.5 Afternoon Dainty version 1, section 1, start pin #

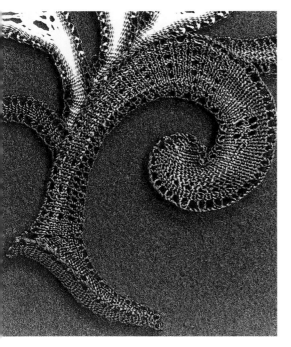

Afternoon Dainty, version 1 (detail). Scroll at beginning of stem and joining of stem to Tenstick section

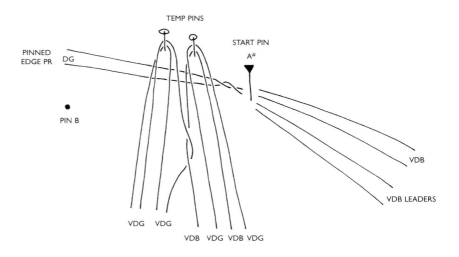

1.6 Afternoon Dainty version 1, section 1, Tenstick colour start

SECTION 2, STEM

Note: Check that pin A# is correctly identified and work is proceeding in the direction indicated (see 1.9).

*START with scroll at pin A#:

Hang 2 prs on pin side by side (see 1.7)

Pin A# is 3rd pin out from scroll centre

Cls tog 2 prs at pin A#

Tw 2 outer edge pr DG

Hang leaders on temp pin

Cls thro inner edge pr VDG

Tw 2 inner edge pr (see 1.8)

Hang 4 prs DG

VDG

VDB

VDG on temp pins, as shown

Note: Temp pins are usually placed outside of work, the pairs hanging in required position. In order to clarify the position of the threads in the diagram the temp pins are shown placed within the work.

Tw 2 leaders

then Cls leaders DG thro 4 prs on temp pins

Place pin a, Tw 2 leaders

Work no change edge st, X T T X T T with leaders and outer edge pr

Remove all temp pins carefully (7 prs)

Work continues by adding pairs, to achieve the order as given when the final pair has been included after pin d

When adding pairs as directed, as far as is possible, place the pairs in their final position, checking their position from the inner edge first (see 1.9)

Add pairs as foll: pin a to pin b, DG
MG

Pin b to pin c, MG
DG

Pin c to pin d, DG
DG

Work a blind pin at pin d, the centre pin of the scroll.

After pin d the thread order must be as foll (single threads):

Inner edge pr 2 x VDG

Leaders 2 x DG

VDG

VDB

VDG

VDB

VDG

3 x DG

3 x MG

DG

MG

5 x DG

VDG

DG

Outer edge pr 2 x DG (13 prs)

After working no change edge st at pin e

Cls leaders thro 1 pr, tie ½ knot

Cls leaders thro 1 more pr, then leave (see 1.10)

Work scroll as foll:

Number passive prs 1–8 (see 1.10)

< Cls passive pr no 1 to outer edge.
Pin

Edge st and return thro 2 prs only, leave >

Repeat < to > with prs no 2–7

Cls passive pr no 8 to outer edge, pin f.

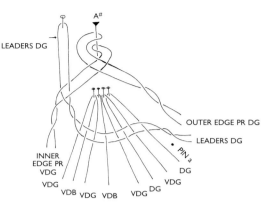

1.8 Afternoon Dainty version 1, section 2, setting up for scroll in colour

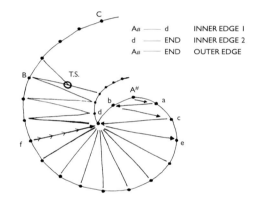

1.9 Afternoon Dainty version 1, section 2, detail of scroll for pin reference

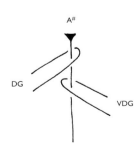

1.7 Afternoon Dainty version 1, section 2, start pin #

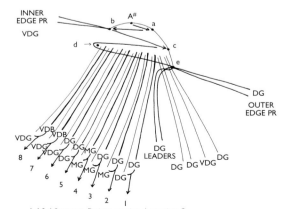

1.10 Afternoon Dainty version 1, section 2, numbering prs for scroll

At pin f:

edge st and return thro all passive prs, to make up blind pin in centre, at pin d

Leaders are now a pr of two single threads VDB

VDG

Change leaders with 1st passive pr DG, X T T X at inner edge. Cont with pr DG as new leaders

Order as foll:

Inner edge pr 2 x VDG

VDG

VDB

New leaders 2 x DG

2 x DG

MG

DG

MG

DG

2 x MG

2 x DG

VDG

DG

VDG

VDB

2 x DG

VDG

DG

Outer edge pr 2 x DG (13 prs)

Cont braid in Cls, do not work any blind pins

When pin B is reached:

work T.S. (X T X T X) with 5th passive pr MG, from inner edge, as 'central pair' (support pins may be used at T.S.)

Work Maltese spot (optional) (see 1.11)

After pin C has been worked:

add 1 pr DB:Pp to become passives 4 and 6, when counting from outer edge

(14 prs)

Work blind pins as required, 5 times in all

If Maltese spot has been omitted, work 1 additional blind pin

After pin D has been worked (see 1.12):

Cls leaders to inner edge, pin and edge st

Change to patt Lattice 1, but keep 1st inner passive pr VDG/VDB at inner edge. This pr will remain next to the edge while the pattern is worked and visually reinforce the design line (14 prs)

At pin E, when braid begins to narrow:

T O & T B, from near inner edge, prs as foll:

VDG/DG

DB: Pp/DG

MG

VDG/DG

MG/DG (9 prs)

Where possible, Cls with neighbouring pr, before T O & T B

Note: When decreasing from near inner edge, keep pattern correct from outer edge. Thicker threads may need to be decreased on each row, whereas finer threads can be decreased on alternate rows.

* *

After pin F:

Cont in patt (9 prs)

When pin B from section 1 is reached:

using top sewings T O outer edge pr DG

Join section 2 to section 1, also using top sewings

Note: When the outer edge pr has been tied, and the leaders sewn in, return leaders thro 1 pr and tie ½ knot (include outer edge pr DG in knot to keep tidy, then T O & T B pr DG).

Return leaders in patt to inner edge

Change to Cls (8 prs)

When braid narrows further, T O & T B 6 prs, from centre of braid, lightest threads first, retaining contrast colours VDB and DB:Pp for a satisfactory blending of colours.

Sew remaining 2 prs, leaders DG and inner edge pr VDG into pin F from section 1.

T O & T B in a bunch to finish.

*

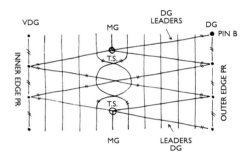

1.11 Afternoon Dainty version 1, section 2, Maltese spot

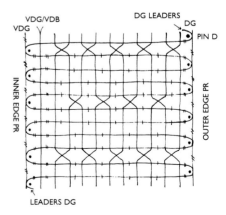

1.12 Afternoon Dainty version 1, section 2, Lattice 1

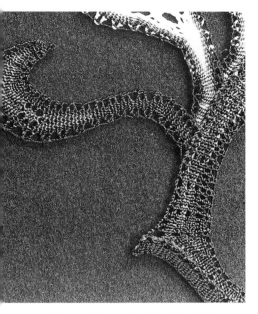

Afternoon Dainty, version 1 (detail). Leaf with pointed start and petal worked with Orchid 1

SECTION 3, LEAF

* START at pin A# (one-colour point start):

Hang 2 prs VDG open around pin A# (see 1.13)

Work false picot: Tw 5, Cls prs tog

Tw 2 outer edge pr only

Hang 1 pr DG leaders on temp pin

Cls leaders DG thro untwisted pr VDG

Tw 2 inner edge pr VDG

Hang 1 pr VDB on temp pin

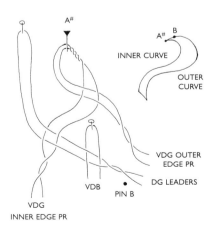

1.13 Afternoon Dainty version 1, section 3, one-colour point start

Cls leaders DG thro 1 pr VDB, Tw 2 leaders

Pin B. Edge st with outer edge pr VDG

Remove temp pins carefully

* * *

Cont in Cls, working blind pins as required,

adding prs to centre of braid as foll to give order as shown to work Maltese spot (see 1.14):

VDB

DG

DG

MG

MG

DG (10 prs)

* * * *

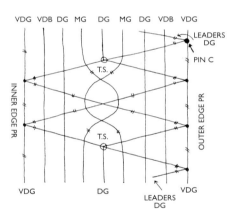

1.14 Afternoon Dainty version 1, section 3, Maltese spot

After pin C:

Cls leaders to centre of braid, make T.S.

Work Maltese spot (see 1.14)

After pin D, where braid narrows:

T O & T B prs from centre of braid, as foll:

DG

MG

MG (7 prs)

* *

After pin E:

Rearrange prs to foll order:

Inner edge pr 2 x VDG

VDB

DG

VDB

2 x DG

VDB

DG

VDB

Outer edge pr 2 x VDG

Leaders 2 x DG

Finish with top sewings into section 2

T O & T B rem few prs in a bunch

*

SECTION 3A, LEAF

Follow instructions for section 3, leaf, from * to *, omitting the rearrangement of threads

Note: Reverse instructions given in diagrams for section 3, as leaf 3a is a mirror image of leaf 3 (see 1.15).

SECTION 4, PETAL

*

Follow instructions for section 3, leaf, from * to * * *, replacing prs with colours as shown (see 1.16).

Note: The inner and outer curves have changed position, therefore:

after false picot, Tw 2 inner edge pr,

after Cls leaders thro untwisted pr,

Tw 2 outer edge pr,

after pin B, edge st with inner edge pr

Cont in Cls adding prs to centre of braid, hanging open around pin, in order as foll:

VDB

Pp

DB:Pp per row

MB

DB:Pp

MB per row

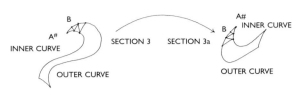

1.15 Afternoon Dainty version 1, sections 3 & 3a, working direction

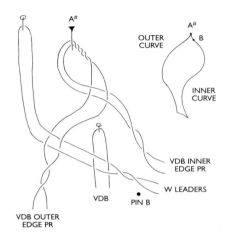

1.16 Afternoon Dainty version 1, section 4, one-colour point start

LB
W
W per row

W
W
W per row

W
W per row (18 prs)
After prs have been added, order must be as foll:
Outer edge pr 2 x VDB
2 x VDB
Pp
DB:Pp
MB
DB:Pp
MB
LB
14 x W
LB

MB
DB:Pp
MB
DB:Pp
Pp
2 x VDB
Inner edge pr 2 x VDB
Leaders 2 x W (18 prs)
* *

After pin C has been worked:
either work ½ st with 5 centre
passive prs
or make T.S. (use support pin) and
start patt Orchid 1 (see 1.17)
Work two sections of patt, make T.S.,
cont in Cls
As braid narrows, T O & T B prs from
centre as foll:
W
W + W
W + W
W
W
LB (10 prs)
Meanwhile, at pin D, change leaders
W to VDG:
Place pin D, (leaders W Tw 2) edge st
Cls thro 1st passive pr
T O & T B old leaders W
Add 1 pr new leaders VDG between
edge pr & 1st passive pr
Cls thro 1st passive pr (again) with
new leaders VDG and cont (see 1.18)
Note: Changing the colour of the
leaders at this point will ensure a
more successful blending of the petal
base into the stem.
Using top sewings, join section 4,
petal, to section 2, stem. Decrease
passive prs when joining sections;
these may also be sewn into section 2,
stem, using top sewings.
T O & T B rem prs in a bunch
*

SECTION 4A, PETAL

Follow instructions for section 4,
petal, from * to *

SECTION 4B, PETAL

Follow instructions for section 4,
petal, from * to *
Note: Work one section of patt only.

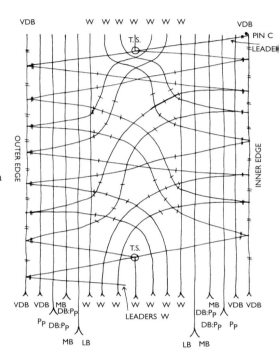

1.17 Afternoon Dainty version 1, sections 4, 4a & 4b Orchid 1

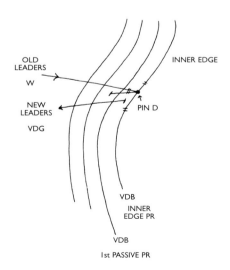

1.18 Afternoon Dainty version 1, section 4, changing colour of leaders

AFTERNOON DAINTY, VERSION 2

Colours: Med Green MG

Dark Green DG

V Dark Green VDG

Cream C

Dark Cream DC

Light Pink LP

Dark Pink DP

Fuschia F

V Dark Red VDR

Techniques: No (colour) change edge stitch

Tenstick colour start

Mixing thread colours

Blind pin

Scroll (colour)

Changing leaders with passive pr

Turning stitch

Top sewings

One-colour round start

Rearranging threads

Changing colour of leaders

Stitches and Braids: Tenstick

Cloth stitch

Maltese spot

Lattice 1

Orchid 1

To Work: Work each section numerically as shown in 1.3 and 1.4. When working version 2 it will be necessary to refer to parts of version 1. No (colour) change edge st is used throughout. Top sewings are used throughout. Colours/threads are shown singly in thread order listings, unless otherwise indicated.

SECTION 1, STEM

Follow instructions for version 1, section 1, stem, from * to * using colours to correspond as foll:

Version 1 > version 2

VDB > VDR

DG > DG

VDG > VDG

START at pin A#:

Hang 3 prs on pin in order VDR

DG

VDR (see 1.19)

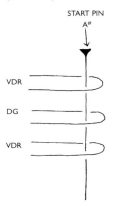

1.19 Afternoon Dainty version 2, section 1, start pin #

After pin B, when all pairs have been added:

L > R order is as foll:

Pinned edge pr 2 x DG

4 x VDG

VDR

VDG

VDR

VDG

Leaders 2 x VDR

Smooth edge pr 2 x VDR

SECTION 2, STEM

Follow instructions for version 1, section 2, stem, from * to * using colours to correspond as foll:

Version 1 > version 2

DG > DG

VDB > VDR

VDG > VDG

MG > MG

DB:Pp > VDR

SECTION 3, LEAF

Note: See additional notes for version 1, section 3, leaf.

* START at pin A# (one-colour round start):

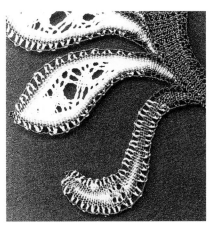

Afternoon Dainty, version 2 (detail). Leaf with rounded start

Note: Although this section is shown worked as an unopened petal in the same threads used for the petal sections 4, 4a and 4b, it is worked in the same way as version 3, section 3, leaf. The only difference being the colour, this section may therefore be worked in the same colourway, as version 3, replacing Pp with VDR.

Hang 2 prs VDR side by side on pin A# (see 1.20)

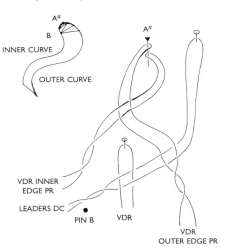

1.20 Afternoon Dainty version 2, section 3, one-colour round start

Cls prs tog. Tw 2 inner edge pr only
Hang 1 pr DC leaders on temp pin
Cls leaders DC thro untwisted pr
VDR
Tw 2 outer edge pr VDR
Hang 1 pr VDR on temp pin
Cls leaders DC thro 1 pr VDR,
Tw 2 leaders
Pin B. Edge st with inner edge pr
VDR
Remove temp pins carefully
* * *

Cont in Cls, working blind pins as
required, also adding prs, hung open
on temp pin, to centre of braid as foll:
F
VDR

F
DP

DP
LP (10 prs)
to give order as shown to work
Maltese spot (see 1.21)
* * * *

After pin C:
Cls leaders to centre of braid

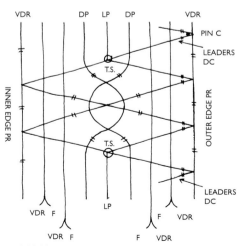

1.21 Afternoon Dainty version 2, section 3, Maltese spot

Make T.S.
Work Maltese spot (see 1.21)

After pin D, where braid narrows:
T O & T B prs from centre of braid,
as foll:
LP
DP
DP (7 prs)
* *

After pin E:
Rearrange pairs to foll order:
Inner edge pr 2 x VDR
VDR
F
VDR
2 x F
VDR
F
VDR
Outer edge pr 2 x VDR
Leaders 2 x DC

At pin F:
Change leaders DC to VDG
Place pin F, (leaders DC Tw 2) edge st
Cls thro 1st passive pr
T O & T B old leaders DC
Add 1 pr new leaders VDG between
edge pr & 1st passive pr
Cls thro 1st passive pr (again) with

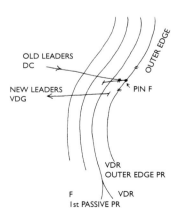

1.22 Afternoon Dainty version 2, section 3, changing colour of leaders

new leaders VDG and cont (see 1.22)
Finish with top sewings into section 2
T O & T B rem few prs in a bunch
*

SECTION 3A, LEAF

Follow instructions for version 2,
section 3, leaf, from * to *, omitting
the rearrangement of threads
Note: Reverse instructions given in
diagrams for section 3, as leaf 3a is a
mirror image of leaf 3 (see 1.23). Also
note that in section 3a, pin F is
worked before pin D. There is no
pin E.

1.23 Afternoon Dainty version 2, sections 3 & 3a, working direction

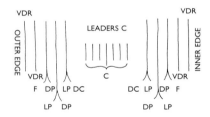

1.24 Afternoon Dainty version 2, sections 4, 4a & 4b, colour map for Orchid 1

SECTIONS 4, 4A & 4B, PETALS

Follow instructions for version 1,
sections 4, 4a & 4b, petals, from * to
* using colours to correspond as foll:
Version 1 > version 2
VDB > VDR
Pp > F
DB:Pp > DP
MB > LP
LB > DC
W > C (see 1.24)

AFTERNOON DAINTY, VERSION 3

Colours: Med Green MG

Dark Green DG

V Dark Green VDG

Purple Pp

Techniques: No (colour) change edge stitch

Tenstick colour start

Mixing thread colours

Blind pin

Scroll (colour)

Changing leaders with passive pr

Turning stitch

Top sewings

One-colour round start

Rearranging threads

Changing colour of leaders

Stitches and Braids: Tenstick

Cloth stitch

Maltese spot

Lattice 1

Orchid 1

To Work: Work each section numerically as shown in 1.3 and 1.4. When working version 3 it will be necessary to refer to parts of version 1. No (colour) change edge st is used throughout. Top sewings are used throughout. Colours/threads are shown singly in thread order listings, unless otherwise indicated.

SECTION 1, STEM

Follow instructions for version 1, section 1, stem, from * to * using colours to correspond as foll:

Version 1 > version 3

VDB > Pp

DG > DG

VDG > VDG

START at pin A#:

Hang 3 prs on pin in order Pp

DG

Pp (see 1.25)

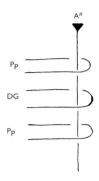

1.25 Afternoon Dainty version 3, section 1, start pin #

After pin B, when all pairs have been added:

L > R order is as foll:

Pinned edge pr 2 x DG

4 x VDG

Pp

VDG

Pp

VDG

Leaders 2 x Pp

Smooth edge pr 2 x Pp

SECTION 2, STEM

Follow instructions for version 1, section 2, stem, from * to * using colours to correspond as foll:

Version 1 > version 3

DG > DG

VDB > Pp

VDG > VDG

MG > MG

DB:Pp > Pp

Note: See also the following notes.

After pin d the thread order must be as foll:

Inner edge pr 2 x VDG

Leaders 2 x DG

VDG

Pp

VDG

Pp

VDG

3 x DG

3 x MG

DG

MG

5 x DG

VDG

DG

Outer edge pr 2 x DG (13 prs)

After scroll has been worked and leaders changed, L > R order is as foll:

Inner edge pr 2 x VDG

VDG

Pp

New leaders 2 x DG

2 x DG

MG

DG

MG

DG

2 x MG

2 x DG

VDG

DG

VDG

Pp

2 x DG

VDG

DG

Outer edge pr 2 x DG (13 prs)

SECTION 3, LEAF

Note: See additional notes for version 1, section 3, leaf.

* START at pin A# (one-colour round start):

Hang 2 prs VDG side by side on pin A# (see 1.26)

Cls prs tog. Tw 2 inner edge pr only

Hang 1 pr DG leaders on temp pin

Cls leaders DG thro untwisted pr

VDG

Tw 2 outer edge pr VDG

Hang 1 pr Pp on temp pin

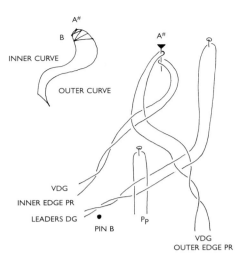

1.28 Afternoon Dainty version 3, sections 3 & 3a, working direction

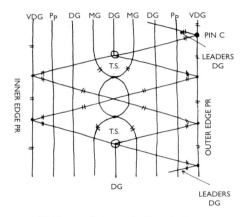

1.26 Afternoon Dainty version 3, section 3, one-colour round start

VDG Pp DG MG DG MG DG Pp VDG

PIN C

LEADERS DG

INNER EDGE PR

T.S.

T.S.

OUTER EDGE PR

DG

LEADERS DG

1.27 Afternoon Dainty version 3, section 3, Maltese spot

Cls leaders DG thro 1 pr Pp, Tw 2 leaders
Pin B. Edge st with inner edge pr VDG
Remove temp pins carefully
* * *

Cont in Cls, working blind pins as required, also adding prs, hung open on temp pin, to centre of braid as foll:
Pp
DG

DG
MG

MG
DG (10 prs)

to give order as shown to work Maltese spot (see 1.27).
* * * *

After pin C:
Cls leaders to centre of braid
Make T.S.
Work Maltese spot (see 1.27)
Cont by foll instructions for version 1, section 3, leaf, from * * * * to * using colours to correspond as foll:
Version 1 > version 3
VDG > VDG
DG > DG
VDB > Pp
MG > MG
*

SECTION 3A, LEAF

Follow instructions for version 3, section 3, leaf, from * to *, omitting the rearrangement of threads
Note: Reverse instructions given in diagrams for section 3, since leaf 3a is a mirror image of leaf 3 (see 1.28). Also note that in section 3a, pin F is worked before pin D. There is no pin E.

SECTIONS 4, 4A & 4B, PETALS

Follow instructions for version 1, sections 4, 4a & 4b, petals, from * to * using colours to correspond as foll:
Version 1 > version 3
VDB > Pp
Pp > VDG
DB:Pp > Pp
MB > VDG
LB > DG
W > MG (see 1.29)
Note: At pin D, change leaders MG to VDG.

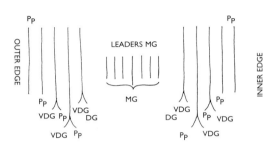

1.29 Afternoon Dainty version 3, sections 4, 4a & 4b, colour map for Orchid 1

AFTERNOON DAINTY, VERSION 4

Colours: Med Green MG
Dark Green DG
V Dark Green VDG
Dark Cream DC
Light Straw Yellow LY
Dark Straw Yellow DY
Light Flesh Pink LFP
Dark Flesh Pink DFP
Olive Green OG

Techniques: No (colour) change edge stitch
Tenstick colour start
Mixing thread colours
Blind pin
Scroll (colour)
Changing leaders with passive pr
Turning stitch
Top sewings
One-colour point start
Two-colour point start
False picot
Rearranging threads
Changing colour of leaders

Stitches and Braids: Tenstick
Cloth stitch
Maltese spot
Lattice 1
Orchid 1

To Work: Work each section
numerically as shown in 1.3. When
working version 4 it will be necessary
to refer to parts of version 1. No
(colour) change edge st is used
throughout. Top sewings are used
throughout. Colours/threads are
shown singly in thread order listings,
unless otherwise indicated.

SECTION 1, STEM

Follow instructions for version 1,
section 1, stem, from * to * using
colours to correspond as foll:
Version 1 > version 4
VDB > OG
DG > DG
VDG > MG
START at pin A#:
Hang 3 prs on pin in order OG
DG
OG (see 1.30)

After pin B, when all pairs have been
added:
L > R order is as foll:
Pinned edge pr 2 x DG
4 x MG
OG
MG
OG
MG
Leaders 2 x OG
Smooth edge pr 2 x OG

SECTION 2, STEM

Follow instructions for version 1,
section 2, stem, from * to * using
colours to correspond as foll:

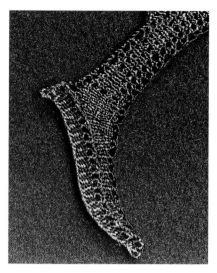

Afternoon Dainty, version 3 (detail). Close-up of the joining of the stem to the Tenstick section, showing raised edge

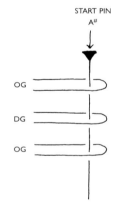

1.30 *Afternoon Dainty version 4, section 1, start pin #*

Version 1 > version 4
DG > MG
VDB > VDG
VDG > DG
MG > OG
DB:Pp > VDG
Note: See also the following
additional notes.
At pin a, after edge st, order is as foll:
Inner edge pr 2 x DG
DG
VDG
DG
VDG
DG

MG
DG
MG
Leaders 2 x MG
Outer edge pr 2 x MG (7prs)
Note: Work continues by adding pairs,
to achieve the order as given when
the final pair has been included after
pin d. When adding pairs as directed,
as far as possible, place the pairs in
their final position, checking their
position from the inner edge first
(see 1.9).
Add pairs as foll:
Pin a to pin b; MG
OG
Pin b to pin c; OG
MG
Pin c to pin d; MG
MG
Work a blind pin at pin d, the centre
pin of the scroll

After pin d the thread order must be
as foll (single threads):
Inner edge pr 2 x DG
Leaders 2 x MG
DG
VDG
DG
VDG
DG
3 x MG
3 x OG
MG
OG
5 x MG
DG
MG
Outer edge pr 2 x MG (13 prs)
After scroll has been worked and
leaders changed, L > R order is as foll:
Inner edge pr 2 x DG
DG
VDG

New leaders 2 x MG

2 x MG

OG

MG

OG

MG

2 x OG

2 x MG

DG

MG

DG

VDG

2 x MG

DG

MG

Outer edge pr 2 x MG (13 prs)

Cont braid in Cls, do not work any

blind pins

When pin B is reached:

Work T.S. with 5th passive pr OG,

from inner edge, as 'central pair'.

(Support pins may be used at T.S.)

Work Maltese spot (optional)

(see 1.31)

At pin E, when braid begins to

narrow:

T O & T B, from near inner edge,

prs as foll:

DG/MG

VDG/MG

DG/MG

VDG/MG

MG (9 prs)

Where possible, Cls with

neighbouring pr, before T O & T B

Note: When decreasing from near

inner edge, keep pattern correct from

outer edge. Thicker threads may need

to be decreased on each row, whereas

finer threads can be decreased on

alternate rows.

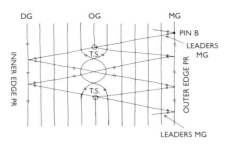

1.31 Afternoon Dainty version 4, section 2,
Maltese spot

SECTION 3, LEAF

Note: See additional notes for version
1, section 3, leaf.
* START at pin A# (one-colour point
start):
Hang 2 prs open around pin A#
(see 1.32)
Work false picot: Tw 5, Cls prs tog
Tw 2 outer edge pr only
Hang 1 pr MG leaders on temp pin
Cls leaders MG thro untwisted pr DG
Tw 2 inner edge pr DG
Hang 1 pr VDG on temp pin
Cls leaders MG thro 1 pr VDG,
Tw 2 leaders
Pin B. Edge st with outer edge pr DG
Remove temp pins carefully
* * *

Cont in Cls, working blind pins as
required, also adding prs to centre of
braid as foll: VDG
MG

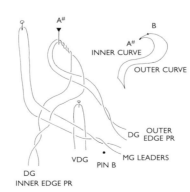

1.32 Afternoon Dainty version 4, section 3,
one-colour point start

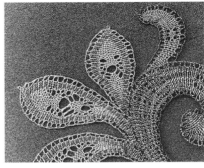

Afternoon Dainty, version 3 (detail). Small leaf with
rounded start and colouring of petals to match the
leaves

MG

OG

OG

MG (10 prs)

to give order as shown to work

Maltese spot (see 1.33).

* * * *

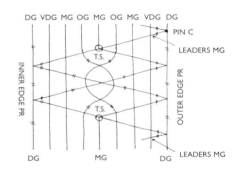

1.33 Afternoon Dainty version 4, section 3,
Maltese spot

After pin C:

Cls leaders to centre of braid

Make T.S.

Work Maltese spot (see 1.33)

Cont by foll instructions for version 1,

section 3, leaf, from * * * * to * using

colours to correspond as foll:

Version 1 > version 4

VDG > DG

DG > MG

VDB > VDG

MG > OG

SECTION 3A, LEAF

This section is omitted in version 4 to allow design to fit an oval frame. If this section is required, follow instructions for version 1, section 3, leaf from * to *, omitting the rearrangement of threads. Use colours as indicated for version 4, section 3. Note: Reverse instructions given in diagrams for section 3, as leaf 3a is a mirror image of leaf 3 (see 1.15).

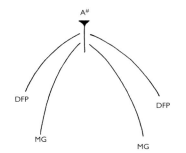

1.34 Afternoon Dainty version 4, sections 4, 4a & 4b, two-colour point start, hanging 2 prs open on pin A#

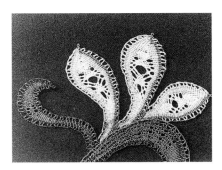

Afternoon Dainty, version 4 (detail). Leaf with pointed start, and petals worked with Orchid 1 showing the different colours at either side of each petal

SECTIONS 4, 4A & 4B, PETALS

*START at pin A# (two-colour point start):

Hang 1 pr MG and 1 pr DFP open around pin A# (see 1.34)

Work false picot: Tw 5, make T.S. (this will ensure that the colours of the edge prs will be in their correct positions), with prs MG and DFP (see 1.35)

Tw 2 inner edge pr DFP only

Hang 1 pr DC leaders on temp pin

Cls leaders thro untwisted pr MG

Tw 2 outer edge pr MG

Hang 1 pr MG and 1 pr DFP on temp pin (see 1.35) side by side, Cls tog

Cls leaders DC thro prs MG & DFP

Tw 2 leaders

Pin B. Edge st with inner edge pr DFP

Remove temp pins carefully

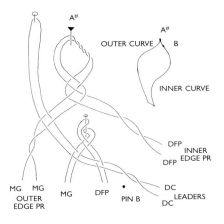

1.35 Afternoon Dainty version 4, sections 4, 4a & 4b, two-colour point start

Cont in Cls adding prs to centre of braid, on temp pin, in order as foll:

Hang side by side: OG
DY per row

Hang staggered: LFP
LY per row

Hang staggered: DY
LY
LY
LY per row

Hang open: DC
DC
DC per row

Hang open: DC
DC per row (18 prs)

After prs have been added, order must be as foll:

Outer edge pr 2 x MG
MG
OG
MG
OG
DY
LY
DY
3 x LY
10 x DC
3 x LY
LFP
LY
LFP
DY
DFP
DY
DFP
Inner edge pr 2 x DFP
Leaders 2 x DC (18 prs)
* *

At pin C:
Follow instructions for version 1, section 4, petal, from * * to * using colours to correspond as foll:
Version 1 > version 4
W > DC
VDG > MG (see 1.36)
Note: See also the following additional notes.
As braid narrows, T O & T B prs from centre as foll:
DC
DC + DC
LY/DC + LY/DC
DC
LY
LY (10 prs)
Meanwhile, at pin D, change leaders DC to MG, (see 1.18)
*

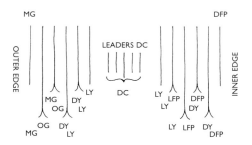

1.36 *Afternoon Dainty version 4, sections 4, 4a &
4b, colour map for Orchid 1*

SECOND THOUGHTS

This motif (see page 47) is worked
similarly, using techniques, stitches
and braids, as illustrated in Afternoon
Dainty, version 1. Any of the other
suggested threads may be used, and
the scale of the pricking adjusted.
Second Thoughts is shown using
Pipers Silks: Spun silk 80/3, Gloss silk
90/3 & Semi-gloss 300.

The differences are that section 1
finishes at the point of the leaf, which
is included in section 1, and there is
(optional) rolled work on sections 1
and 2. Section 3 is worked in ½ st
instead of Orchid 1.

Pricking Size: See 1.37.
100%: See Pricking notes for
Afternoon Dainties.

Thread: See Thread notes for
Afternoon Dainties.

Colours: Med Green MG
Dark Green DG
V Dark Green VDG
White W
Light Blue LB
Med Blue MB
Dark Blue:Purple DB:Pp
V Dark Blue VDB
Purple Pp

Techniques: No (colour) change edge
stitch

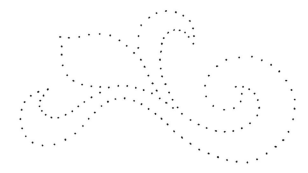

1.37 *Second Thoughts, pricking*

Mixing thread colours
Blind pin
Scroll (colour)
Changing leaders with passive pr
Turning stitch
Top sewings
Roll (Withof)
One-colour point start
False picot
Rearranging threads
Changing colour of leaders

Stitches and Braids: Cloth stitch
Lattice 1
Maltese spot
½ stitch

To Work: Work each section
numerically as shown in 1.39. When
working Second Thoughts it will be
necessary to refer to parts of
Afternoon Dainty, version 1. See pin
reference plan (1.38). No (colour)
change edge st is used throughout.
Top sewings are used throughout.
Colours/threads are shown singly in
thread order listings, unless otherwise
indicated.
Rolled work: At the tip of the leaf,
section 1, the work can either be
finished in the usual way, or the
threads may be rolled (Withof roll)
back along the outer edge of section 1
to finish in the centre of the scroll.

When section 2 has joined section 1,
threads may also be rolled (Withof
roll) back along the inner curve of
section 2 to the tip of the leaf (1.39,
2.10, 2.11, 2.12).

SECTION 1, STEM/LEAF

Follow instructions for Afternoon
Dainty, version 1, section 2, stem,
from * to * *
Note: In this design, the optional
Maltese spot has been omitted,
therefore there is no pin B.

After pin F:
Cont in patt

After pin G:
Change to Cls, the thread order must
be as foll:
Inner edge pr 2 x VDG
Leaders 2 x DG
VDG

VDB
VDG
VDB
DB:Pp
5 x DG
MG
DG
Outer edge pr 2 x DG (9 prs)

At each of pins H, I and J:
Add 1 pr DG, to be placed within the

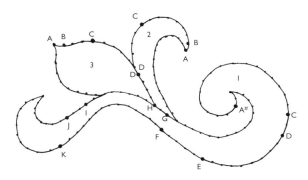

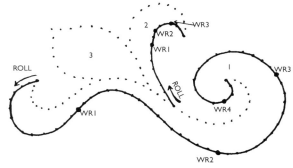

1.38 Second Thoughts, pin reference plan

1.39 Second Thoughts, order of working and rolled edges

group of 5 x DG passive threads

At pin K:
Work a Maltese spot, using the central
pr to make T.S.
Finish to a point, T O & T B prs from
centre of braid
Either T B rem prs in a bunch
or roll (Withof), back along the outer
edge to scroll centre (see 1.39)
To roll: Follow instructions for rolling
back, Fishtails, pin S (see 2.33, 2.34 &
2.36)
Use 1 x DG as leader to roll around
threads in roll as foll:
2 x VDG
1 x VDB
2 x DG
1 x MG
1 x DB:Pp (1 + 7 threads)
At pin WR 1, T B 1 thread MG
from roll
At pin WR 2, T B 1 thread DG
from roll

At pin WR 3, T B 1 thread VDG
from roll
At pin WR 4, T B 1 thread DG
from roll
Finish by top sewing rem threads into
scroll centre
Note: When working a rolled section,
threads within the roll may be

increased or decreased and the colours
changed, as dictated by the effect..

SECTION 2, LEAF (SEE 1.38)

Follow instructions for version 1,
section 3, leaf, from * to *, omitting
the rearrangement of threads

*Second Thoughts, worked in white with rolled edge.
Madeira Tanne 30 (cotton)*

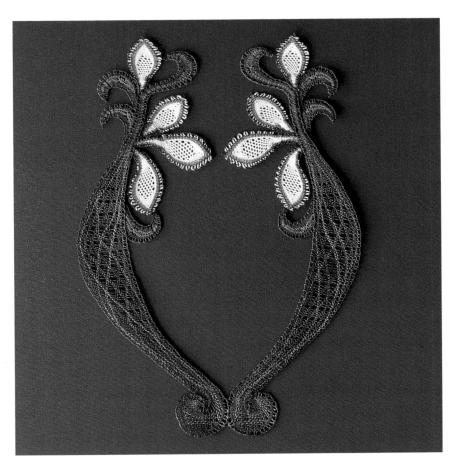

Afterthoughts. Pipers Silks 80/3 and 90/3

1.40 Afterthoughts, pricking

Note: Reverse instructions given in diagrams for section 3, as leaf 3a is a mirror image of leaf 3 (see 1.15).

Join section 2 to section 1 using top sewings

Optional: Roll (Withof), back along the inner curve, to the tip of the leaf (see 1.39).

Use 1 x VDG as leader, to roll as foll:

1 x VDG

I x VDB

3 x DG (1 + 5 threads)

At pin WR 1, T B 1 thread DG from roll

At pin WR 2, T B 1 thread DG from roll

At pin WR 3, T B 1 thread DG from roll

Finish by top sewing rem threads into tip of leaf

Section 3, Petal

Follow instructions for Afternoon Dainty, version 1, section 4b, petal, from * to *.

Instead of Orchid 1, ½ st (optional) has been worked

AFTERTHOUGHTS

Afterthoughts also uses in a similar way the techniques, stitches and braids from Afternoon Dainties and Second Thoughts.

The design is shown worked as a mirror image of the motif, but if preferred the motif may be worked singly. Alternatively, the mirror-image design could be 'opened out' so that the two scrolls meet at the centre (using different pinholes) to form a long, narrow design.

The double (twice worked) scroll is a useful technique that makes an appearance in this motif. When working a scroll (based on the

Milanese scroll, used for the Afternoon Dainties and Second Thoughts) in colour, it is noticeable that the coloured threads which on the whole were at the left side of the braid, are, when the scroll is completed, now at the right side. When this scroll technique is worked twice (double scroll) the coloured threads return to their original position. Thus, when working in colour, this very useful technique can be employed in order to manipulate threads.

The pattern Lattice 1 is used to great effect in Afterthoughts, where the plotted movement of threads can be readily observed at the widening of the braid in section 1. In the previous designs, the movement of the threads, and therefore the colours, has been achieved in exactly the same way but less noticeably since the braids were narrower and the threads more densely placed.

There is no rolled work illustrated in Afterthoughts, but any of the edges could be rolled. The double scroll would be rolled as a Withof rolled scroll. As in Second Thoughts, the petals are worked in ½ st instead of Orchid 1.

Any of the suggested threads for the Afternoon Dainties may be used, with the appropriate adjustments made to the scale of the pricking. In the example illustrated, Pipers Silks were used: Spun silk 80/3, Gloss silk 90/3 & Semi-gloss 300.

Pricking Size: See 1.40.

100%: See Pricking notes for Afternoon Dainties

Thread: See Thread notes for Afternoon Dainties

Colours: Med Green MG

Dark Green DG

V Dark Green VDG

White W

Light Blue LB

Med Blue MB

Dark Blue:Purple DB:Pp

V Dark Blue VDB

Purple Pp

Techniques: No (colour) change edge stitch

Mixing thread colours

Blind pin

Double scroll (2 x worked, colour)

Closed scroll

Changing leaders with passive pr

Turning stitch

Top sewings

Side sewings

One-colour point start

False picot

Rearranging threads

Changing colour of leaders

Stitches and Braids: Cloth stitch

Lattice 1

Maltese spot

½ stitch

To Work: Work each section numerically as shown in 1.41. When working Afterthoughts it will be necessary to refer to parts of Afternoon Dainty, version 1. No (colour) change edge st is used throughout. Top sewings are used throughout, except when joining the two scrolls tog (section 1a is joined to section 1 with side sewings). Colours/threads are shown singly in thread order listings, unless otherwise indicated.

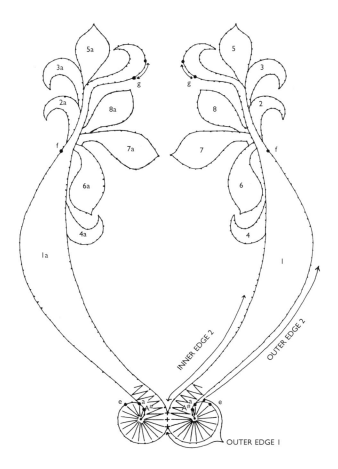

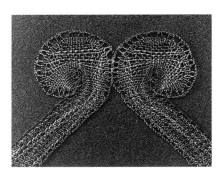

Afterthoughts (detail). Double scrolls and the joining of both sections without throwing back the edge pair

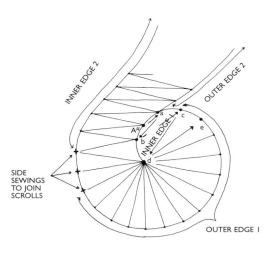

1.41 Afterthoughts, pin reference plan and order of working

1.42 Afterthoughts, detail of scroll, pin reference plan

SECTION 1, STEM/LEAF

Follow instructions for Afternoon Dainty, version 1, section 2, stem, from * to pin e

START at pin A# (see 1.42)

To work double (2 x worked) scroll, which in this design is also a closed scroll, (see also 2.95 & 2.96):

Work scroll as far as passive pr no7

Work scroll for 1st time (see 1.10), number prs

Take passive pr no 7 VDB/VDG thro all passives to make up blind pin, pin d, in centre

Return to outer edge. Pin

Edge st and return thro 2 prs

Now scroll is worked for 2nd time (number prs as before)

Take passive pr no 6 DG as new leaders to cont in Cls

As this double (2 x worked) scroll is also a closed scroll (see 2.95 & 2.96), untwist previous edge pr remaining at centre (blind) pin and include as a passive pr

Cont in Cls (omit Maltese spot after scroll), joining this part of the braid to the previously worked scroll edges with top sewings at pins b, A# & a (see 1.42)

Thread order must be L > R as foll:

Previous inner edge 1, 2 x VDG

VDG

VDB

2 x DG

VDG

VDB

VDG

3 x DG

3 x MG

DG

MG

3 x DG

VDG

DG

Inner edge 2, 2 x DG

Leaders 2 x DG (13 prs) (see 1.42)

After 1st sewing into scroll edge has been made at pin b, add 1 pr DB:Pp, to become passives 6 and 8, when

Afterthoughts (detail). Movement of threads and changing from braid, Lattice 1 to cloth st. Leaf with Maltese spot and ½ st petals

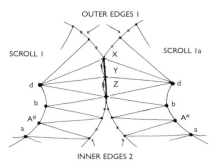

1.43 Afterthoughts, detail of the joining of scrolls, using side sewings

counting from (new) outer edge 2 (14 prs)

After 2nd sewing has been made at pin A#, start patt Lattice 1 (see Afternoon Dainty, version 1, section 2, stem)

Note: Use 6 sets of 2 prs Cls tog to start patt.

At pin a:

Make top sewing, but also as this is a closed scroll, add 1 pr VDG, to become edge pr of outer edge 2 (15 prs)

Cont in patt to pin f

After pin f:

Change to Cls

Work 1 row,

L > R order as foll:

Outer edge 2, 2 x VDG

2 x VDG

{DG} 2nd pr to be

{DB:Pp} T O & T B

VDG

VDB

{VDG} 4th pr to be

{VDB} T O & T B

DG

DB:Pp

Centre pr 2 x DG

{VDG} 5th pr to be

{DG} T O & T B

MG

DG

{2 x MG} 1st pr T O & T B

{2 x DG} 3rd pr T O & T B

MG

DG

VDG

DG

Inner edge 2, 2 x DG

Leaders 2 x DG (15 prs)

T O & T B prs as listed, in order indicated, 1 pr per row (10 prs)

Note: If, while working the narrow part of section, passives become too compressed, T O & T B additional prs from centre. However, as braid widens, they must be replaced in order well before working the Maltese spot at the leaf end of the section.

After pin g (see 1.41):

Work Maltese spot (see 1.14).

Finish in the usual way:

T O & T B prs from centre as braid narrows

Tie back rem few prs in a bunch and secure to work

SECTION 1A, STEM/LEAF (MIRROR IMAGE OF SECTION 1)

Follow instructions for section 1

* to *

Note: Join to previously worked section 1 with side sewings (see 1.43).

When making side sewings, it is not necessary to T O & T B the outer edge pr; Tw 2 or 3 times this outer edge pr after making side sewing at pin X.

Cont working scroll

When leaders return to pin Y:

Make side sewing in the usual way but place the twisted outer edge pr between the leaders after making the sewing, then Tw 2 leaders and cont with scroll

Tw 2 or 3 times, the outer edge pair again

When leaders return to pin Z:

Make sewing as before and place twisted outer edge pr between leaders, Tw 2 leaders and cont

Tw 2 or 3 times, the outer edge pr again

Cont as normal.

Note: When working section 1a, the edge at which the patt commences must be reversed, to ensure an exact mirror image of section 1.

SECTIONS 2, 2A, 3, 3A, 4, & 4A, LEAVES

Follow instructions for Afternoon Dainty, version 1, sections 3 & 3a

SECTIONS 5, 5A, 6, 6A, 7, 7A, 8 & 8A, PETALS

Follow instructions for Afternoon Dainty, version 1, sections 4, 4a & 4b

At pin C, either patt Orchid 1 or ½ st may be worked

When the petal narrows, change to Cls, then change the leaders to VDG, before T O & T B prs from centre of braid, making a blind pin near the base of the petal and making top sewings into existing green sections.

MORNING GLORY AND BUDDING GLORY

Both of the Glory patterns are designs that continue to build upon the painterly use of colour explored previously, and refer to the instructions given for Afternoon Dainty, version 1.

The main stem, section 1, starts in exactly the same way as Afternoon Dainty, section 2, stem, but continues, decreasing in size, to give the effect of its recession into the background. To give a satisfactory composition to the finished piece, the Morning Glory is worked twice, once in reverse, as can be seen in the illustration overleaf. The perspective is further enhanced by allowing the colours of the threads, with a small amount of manipulation, to indicate the sunlight playing on the edges of the stem. The positioning of the threads when commencing the Milanese braid, Lattice 1, is important, since the threads are allowed to take their prescribed course, which directs the different colours to describe light and shade.

The addition of the bud and tendril, sections 5 & 6, of Budding Glory, provides the necessary balance to the design if only one Glory is to be worked. Only the positioning of the coloured threads and their careful shading describes the twisting form of the bud, since it is worked entirely in cloth stitch.

The way in which the side sections of the flower, sections 4a & 4b, are started will allow the work to proceed using the shading to indicate the edge curl of the flower. Pairs are added, whilst others are set aside to be used later. The working direction of these two sections is changed by using a variation of the scroll method in a way that will keep the shading exactly in place.

Pricking Size: See 1.44
100%: Both versions; see Pricking notes for Afternoon Dainties

Thread: See thread chart 1.1; also refer to Thread notes given for Afternoon Dainties. As mentioned in the notes at the beginning of the chapter, it is advisable to use only the instructions for the blue or red motifs. To make sense of the design if using red, the leaf, section 2, must be worked using the same colour order given for Afternoon Dainty, version 3, section 3, leaf.

1.44 Morning Glory & Budding Glory, pricking

1.45 Morning Glory & Budding Glory, order of working

MORNING GLORY

Colours: Med Green MG
Dark Green DG
V Dark Green VDG
White W
Light Blue LB
Med Blue MB
Dark Blue:Purple DB:Pp
V Dark Blue VDB
Purple Pp

Techniques: No (colour) change
   edge stitch
Mixing thread colours
Blind pin
Scroll (colour)
Changing leaders with passive pr
Turning stitch
Top sewings
One-colour point start
False picot

Rearranging threads
Changing colour of leaders (exchange
   of edge pr and leaders)
Changing edge prs (3 variations)
Changing braid to Tenstick
Changing Tenstick to braid
Changing Tenstick edge
Scroll method (variation, with
   controlled hole)
Discarding prs to be collected later
Colour shading (Budding Glory, bud)
Tenstick colour point start (Budding
Glory, tendril)

Stitches and Braids: Cloth stitch
Maltese spot
Lattice 1
Tenstick
Orchid 1

To Work: Work each section
numerically as shown in 1.45. No
(colour) change edge st is used
throughout. Top sewings are used
throughout. Colour/threads are shown
singly in thread order listings, unless
otherwise indicated. When working
reverse motif, turn diagrams upside-
down.

SECTION 1, STEM (SEE 1.46)

Follow instructions for Afternoon
Dainty, section 2, stem, from
* to * *

* *

After pin F:
Continue in patt Lattice 1 (9 prs)
When braid begins to widen, add 1 pr
VDG at pins G, H, & I (to become
passives 1 & 3 from outer curve edge)
(12 prs)

At pin J:
Exchange outer loop edge pr VDG
with leaders DG, to become leaders
VDG and outer loop edge pr DG thus:
Tw 2 leaders, pin
Cls prs tog and Tw 2 both prs
(see 1.47)

At pin K:
Change edge prs at inner loop 1 edge
thus:
Work around blind pin K, 1st time
with leaders VDG
Add 1 pr VDG to become passives
1 & 2 from inner loop edge
Work back to outer loop edge, leave

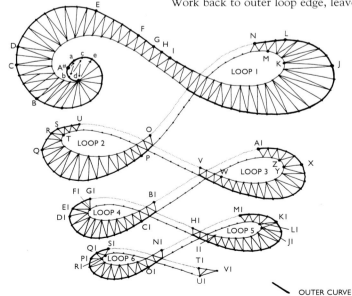

1.46 Morning Glory & Budding Glory, pin reference plan, section 1

OUTER CURVE

INNER CURVE

TENSTICK

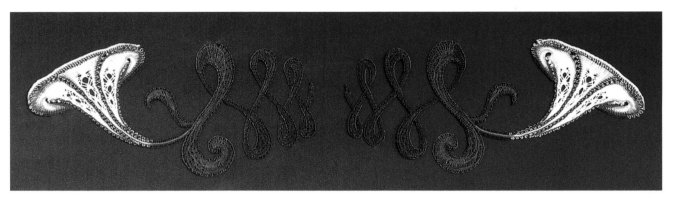

Morning Glory. Gutermann Silk S 303

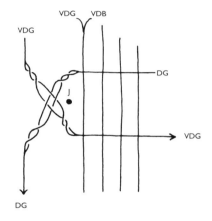

1.47 Morning Glory & Budding Glory section 1, exchanging outer loop pr with leaders

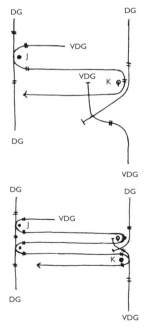

1.48a & 1.48b Morning Glory & Budding Glory section 1, changing edge prs

At the inner loop edge, Cls edge pr DG thro added passive pr VDG T O & T B pr DG. Tw 2 pr VDG (see 1.48a)
Collect leaders from outside loop edge, work to inner loop edge, make up blind pin K and cont in patt (see 1.48a and 1.48b)

After pin L, when braid narrows:
T O & T B prs DG
DG
MG/VDG
DG/DB:Pp
DG/VDG (7prs)

At pin M:
Change to Cls
Add 1 pr VDG to ensure single passive threads 1, 2, 3, 4 at outer loop edge are all VDG (8 prs)

After pin N:
Change to Tenstick thus:
< Untwist edge pr DG and Cls thro 1st passive pr, T O & T B pr D G Cont in Tenstick > (see 1.49)
Leaders VDG
(7 prs rem: 12 single threads VDG 2 single threads VDB)
When working Tenstick, the braids will cross, use top sewings to join

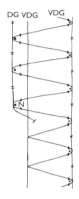

1.49 Morning Glory & Budding Glory section 1, changing braid to Tenstick

At pin O:
Work edge st and leave leaders VDG at edge
Add inner loop 2 edge pr DG thus:
< Add 1 pr DG (to be 2nd passive pr from inner loop edge)
Cls pr DG and 1st passive pr VDG tog Tw 2 pr DG (new inner edge pr)
Collect leaders and work to inner loop edge >
Tw 2, pin and edge st (X T T X T T)
Cont in Cls
Add 1 pr DG to become passives 2 & 4 from inner loop edge
Add 1 pr DG to become passives 5 & 7 from inner loop edge (see 1.50)
(10 prs)

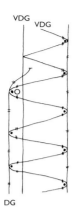

1.50 Morning Glory & Budding Glory section 1, changing Tenstick to braid

After pin P:
Work to inner loop 2 edge
Change back to patt

At pin Q:
Change outer loop 2 edge pr VDG to
DG thus:
< Hang 1 pr DG on temp pin
Untwist outer loop edge pr VDG
Cls prs DG and VDG tog. Tw 2 pr
DG (new outer loop edge pr),
pin Q and edge st
Remove temp pin. T O & T B pr
VDG (see 1.51) >

At pin R:
Change to Cls

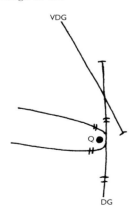

1.51 Morning Glory & Budding Glory section 1, changing outer loop edge prs

After pin S:
T O & T B, 1 pr DG/VDG and 1 pr
DG/VDB, at the same time:

At pin T:
Change inner loop 2 edge pr DG to
VDG thus:
< Work 2nd time to blind pin
Tw 2 Leaders VDG, pin T
Cls Leaders VDG and inner loop edge
pr DG tog
Tw 2 both prs (now the leaders are
DG, and the new inner loop edge pr is
VDG)
Cls leaders DG thro 1st passive pr
VDG
T O & T B leaders DG
Use 1st passive pr VDG as new
leaders (see 1.52) (7 prs) >
Note: Exchange any remaining
passives DG/VDG for VDG thus: Cls
added prs VDG thro DG/VDG prs.

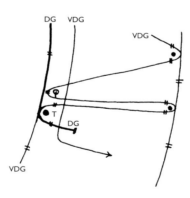

1.52 Morning Glory & Budding Glory section 1, changing inner loop edge prs

T O & T B DG/VDG prs.

At pin U:
Change to Tenstick
Follow instructions for pin N
(see 1.49)
Leaders VDG
Note: When one of the leading
threads is VDB, exchange it with the

1st inner passive VDG.
(6 prs rem: 11 single threads VDG
1 single thread VDB)
Join crossing braids as before.

At pin V:
Work edge st and leave leaders VDG
at edge
Add inner loop 3 edge pr DG: follow
instructions for pin O (see 1.50)
Cont in Cls
Add 1 pr DG, to become passives 2 &
4, from inner loop edge (8 prs)

After pin W:
Work to outer loop 3 edge, change
back to patt

At pin X:
Change outer loop 3 edge pr VDG to
DG
Follow pin Q instructions (see 1.51)

At pin Y:
Change inner loop 3 edge pr DG to
VDG
Follow pin T instructions (see 1.52)

At pin Z:
Change to Cls

At pin A1:
Change to Tenstick
Follow instructions for pin N
(see 1.49)
Leaders VDG
Note: When one of the leading
threads is VDB, exchange it with the
1st inner passive VDG.
(6 prs rem: 11 single threads VDG
1 single thread VDB)
Join crossing braids as before
At pin B1:
Work edge st and leave leaders VDG
at edge

Add inner loop 4 edge pr DG
Follow instructions for pin O
(see 1.50)
Cont in Cls (7 prs)

After pin C1:
Work to inner loop 4 edge
Change back to patt

At pin D1:
Change outer loop 4 edge pr VDG to
DG
Follow instructions for pin Q
(see 1.51)

At pin E1:
Change to Cls

At pin F1:
Change inner loop 4 edge pr DG to
VDG
Follow instuctions for pin T (see 1.52)
Note: Move passive thread VDB to
become 1st passive at pinned edge.

At pin G1:
Change to Tenstick
Follow instructions for pin N
(see 1.49).
Leaders VDG
(5 prs rem: 9 single threads VDG
1 single thread VDB)
Join crossing braids as before

At pin H1:
Work edge st and leave leaders VDG
at edge
Add inner loop 5 edge pr DG
Follow instructions for pin O
(see 1.50)

After pin I1:
Work to inner loop 5 edge
Change back to patt
Note: There are only two prs rem in

patt and it is therefore not possible to
Cls two separate prs instead, Tw 1
each pr (see 1.53).

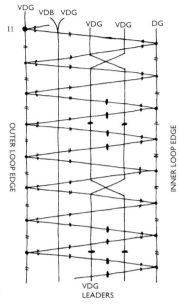

1.53 Morning Glory & Budding Glory section 1, Lattice 1 variation, working with only two pattern prs

At pin J1:
Change inner loop 5 edge pr DG to
VDG
Follow instructions for pin T
(see 1.52)
Add 1 pr VDG to become passives
1 & 3 from inner loop edge (6 prs)

At pin K1:
Change outer loop 5 edge pr VDG to
DG
Follow instructions for pin Q
(see 1.51)

At pin L1:
Change to Cls

At pin M1:
Change to Tenstick
Follow instructions for pin N
(see 1.49)
Leaders VDG

(5 prs rem: 9 single threads VDG
1 single thread VDB)
Note: Move passive thread VDB to
become 1st passive at pinned edge.

At pin N1:
Work edge st and leave leaders VDG
at edge
Add inner loop 6 edge pr DG
Follow instructions for pin O
(see 1.50)

After pin O1:
Work to inner loop 6 edge
Change back to patt (see 1.53)

At pin P1:
Change outer loop 6 edge pr VDG to
DG
Follow instructions for pin Q
(see 1.51)

At pin Q1:
Change to Cls

At pin R1:
Change inner loop 6 edge pr DG to
VDG
Follow instructions for pin T
(see 1.52)

At pin S1:
Change to Tenstick
Follow instructions for pin N
(see 1.49)
Leaders VDG
(4 prs rem: 7 single threads VDG
1 single thread VDB)

At pin T1:
Change Tenstick edge thus:
< Before placing pin T1, Tw 2
non-pinned passive edge pr
Work leaders thro 1st passive pr next
to previously pinned edge

Tw 2 leaders, pin & edge st with previously unpinned passive edge pr
Untwist previously pinned edge pr >
Cont in Tenstick, the pinned edge is now on the opposite side of the work (see 1.54)

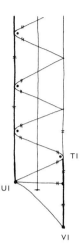

1.54 Morning Glory & Budding Glory section 1, changing sides of Tenstick pinned edge and the finish of section 1

At pin U1:
Work blind pin, using pin U1 as a support (see 1.54)

At pin V1:
To finish, after the last pin has been worked, T O & T B prs in a bunch (see 1.54)

SECTION 2, LEAF
Follow instructions for Afternoon Dainty, version 1, section 3, leaf (see 1.3)

SECTION 3, FLOWER RIM (SEE 1.56)
START at pin A#:
Hang 3 prs on pin in order LB
DB:Pp
LB (see 1.55)
Cls Inner (pinned) edge pr LB thro pr

DB:Pp
Tw 2 pr DB:Pp
Work Tenstick smooth edge with both prs LB (X T X T X)
Leaders and smooth edge pr are both LB

Before pin B is worked:
Add 1 pr DB:Pp
1 pr MB
1 pr MB
1 pr W
1 pr W (8 prs)

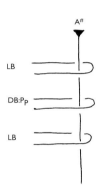

1.55 Morning Glory & Budding Glory section 3, start pin A#

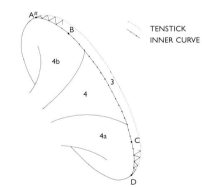

1.56 Morning Glory & Budding Glory section 3, pin reference plan

to give order as foll:
Inner edge pr 2 x DB:Pp
DB:Pp
MB
DB:Pp
2 x MB
W
MB
3 x W
Smooth edge pr 2 x LB
Leaders 2 x LB (8 prs)

After pin C has been worked:
T O & T B prs as foll:
1 pr W
1 pr W/MB
1 pr W/MB
1 pr MB/DB:Pp
1 pr MB/DB:Pp (3 prs)

At pin D:
To finish, T O & T B rem 3 prs in a bunch, using previously T O & T B prs to secure to work

SECTION 4, FLOWER (SEE 1.57)
Using top sewings into pinned edge of section 3, hang on 27 prs in single thread order as foll:
Edge pr 2 x VDB
2 x VDB
2 x Pp
2 x DB:Pp
2 x MB
2 x MB
2 x LB
2 x LB
22 x W
2 x LB
2 x LB
2 x MB
2 x MB
2 x DB:Pp
2 x Pp

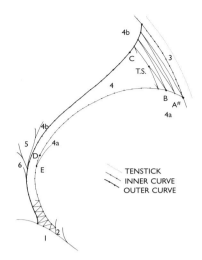

TENSTICK
INNER CURVE
OUTER CURVE

1.57 Morning Glory & Budding Glory section 4, pin reference plan

Morning Glory (detail). Flower worked with Orchid 1

2 x VDB

Edge pr 2 x VDB

Note: Hang each of the edge prs on the pinholes at the edge of section 4. Hang the remaining prs at 2 prs per pinhole, but hanging the central pr W and 2 other prs W from temp pins above work.

Rearrange threads to obtain single thread order as foll:

Edge pr 2 x VDB

VDB

Pp

VDB

Pp

DB:Pp

MB

DB:Pp

2 x MB

LB

MB

2 x LB

W

LB

20 x W

LB

W

2 x LB

MB

LB

2 x MB

DB:Pp

MB

DB:Pp

Pp

VDB

Pp

VDB

Edge pr 2 x VDB (27 prs)

Start at pin A#:

Add leaders W, using top sewing, into same bar as edge pr, to hang between inner curve edge pr VDB and 1st passive pr Pp/VDB (28 prs)

Tw 3 both edge prs VDB

Cls leaders to outer curve edge, work edge st and cont in Cls (see 1.57)

After pin B has been worked:

Cls to centre, make T.S. with centre pr W using support pin (see 1.57)

Start patt Orchid 1 (see 1.17)

Follow instructions given for Afternoon Dainty, version 1, section 4, petal

Work 3 patt repeats

After pin C, when braid narrows:

Cont in patt

T O & T B prs from each side evenly as foll:

2 x W/LB

2 x LB/MB

2 x LB/MB

2 x MB/DB:Pp

2 x Pp/VDB

2 x W (16 prs)

After 3rd patt section has been worked, Cls to centre, make T.S. and cont in Cls

T O & T B 7 prs W from centre (9 prs)

Cont in Cls, order as foll:

Edge pr 2 x VDB

VDB

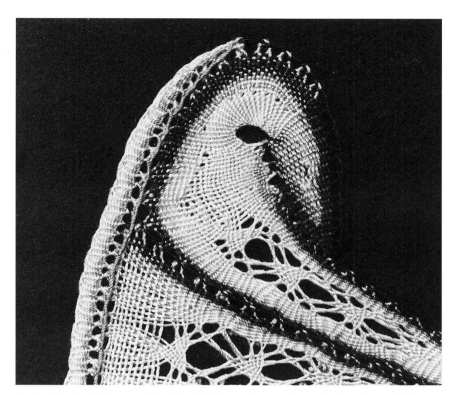

Morning Glory (detail). Flower worked with Orchid 1, joining of flower sections and working of a controlled hole

SECTION 4A, FLOWER (SEE 1.58)

START at pin A#:

Hang on 2 prs VDBa & VDBb (see 1.59)

Cls prs tog, Tw 2 pr VDBa (outer edge 1 pr)

Hang 1 pr leaders VDBc on temp pin

Cls leaders VDBc thro untwisted pr VDBb

Tw 2 pr VDBb (see 1.59)

Set this pr VDBb aside to the back of work to become the edge pr at outer

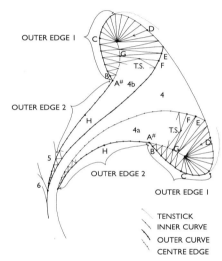

1.58 Morning Glory & Budding Glory section 4a & 4b, pin reference plan

Pp

DB:Pp

MB

LB

2 x W

LB

MB

DB:Pp

Pp

VDB

Edge pr 2 x VDB

Leaders 2 x W (9 prs)

After pin D has been worked:

Add 2 prs VDG to become passives 2 & 4 from inner curve edge and outer curve edge

T O & T B, 1 pr W

1 pr LB

At pin E:

Change leaders W to VDG

Follow instructions as given for

Afternoon Dainty, version 1, section 4, petal (see 1.18)

Order is as foll:

Edge pr 2 x VDB

VDB

VDG

Pp

VDG

DB:Pp

2 x MB

DB:Pp

VDG

Pp

VDG

VDB

Edge pr 2 x VDB

Leaders 2 x VDG (9 prs)

To finish, join to sections 1 & 2 using top sewings

T O & T B in a bunch

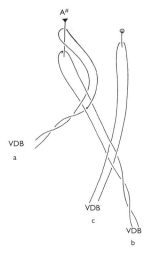

1.59 Morning Glory & Budding Glory section 4a, start

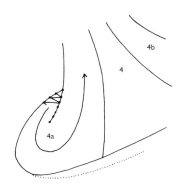

1.60 *Morning Glory & Budding Glory section 4a, working direction*

edge 2 (see 1.61)

Remove temp pin

Note: The direction of working this section changes (see 1.60).

Hang 2 prs VDB and 2 prs Pp on temp pin (see 1.61), above and between pin A# and pin B, in single thread order as foll:

VDB

Pp

VDB

2 x Pp

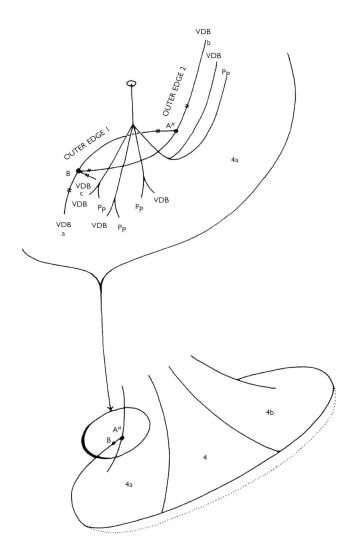

1.61 *Morning Glory & Budding Glory section 4a, setting up prs and working pin A# to pin B*

VDB

Pp

VDB

Tw 1 tog central pr Pp

Cls leaders VDBc thro 1st passive pr VDB/Pp

Set this pr VDB/Pp aside next to pr VDBb (see 1.61)

Cls leaders VDBc thro 3 rem passive prs, Tw 2

Pin B, edge st at outer edge 1

Remove temp pin (7 prs)

Note: There are now 2 prs set aside, outer edge 2 pr VDBb and passive pr VDB/Pp. Cont working with rem 3 passive prs, leader pr and outer edge 1 pr.

Cont in Cls

Note: When working the following sequence, as far as pin C, the nos of passive prs given do not include prs set aside, leader pr or outer edge 1 pr.

Cls to centre edge, add 2 prs, VDB & Pp, in order, from outer edge 1, VDB, Pp, Pp, VDB, to become passive prs 3 & 4 from outer edge 1

Tw 2 leaders, pin, do not edge st

Set aside extreme centre edge pr VDB/Pp (4 passive prs)

Cls to outer edge 1, add 2 prs, VDB & Pp, in order, from outer edge 1, VDB, Pp, VDB, Pp, to become passive prs 4 & 5 from outer edge 1

Tw 2 leaders, pin, edge st (6 passive prs)

Cls to centre edge, add 2 prs, DB:Pp to become passive prs 4 & 5 from outer edge 1

Tw 2 leaders, pin, do not edge st

Set aside extreme centre edge pr VDB/Pp (7 passive prs)

Cls to outer edge 1, add 2 prs, DB:Pp
& MB, in order from outer edge 1,
DB:Pp, MB, DB:Pp, MB, to become
passive prs 4 & 5 from outer edge 1
Tw 2 leaders, pin, edge st
(9 passive prs)

Cls to centre edge, add 1 pr MB, to
become passive pr 6 from outer edge 1
Tw 2 leaders, pin, do not edge st
Set aside extreme centre edge pr
VDB/Pp (9 passive prs)

Cls to outer edge 1, add 1 pr MB, to
become passive pr 7 from outer edge 1
Tw 2 leaders, pin, edge st
(10 passive prs)

Cls to centre edge, add 2 prs LB, to
become single passives 11, 13, 15, 17,
from outer edge 1
Tw 2 leaders, pin, do not edge st
Set aside extreme centre edge pr
VDB/Pp (11 passive prs)

Cls to outer edge 1, add 2 prs, LB &
W, in order from outer edge 1, LB, W,
LB, W to become single passives 13,
14, 15, 16, from outer edge 1
Tw 2 leaders, pin, edge st
(13 passive prs)

Cls to centre edge, add 1 pr W, to
become passive pr 8 from outer edge 1
Tw 2 leaders, pin, do not edge st
Set aside extreme centre edge pr
DB:Pp (13 passive prs)

Cls to outer edge 1, add 1 pr W, to
become single passives 16, 17, from
outer edge 1
Tw 2 leaders, pin, do not edge st
(14 passive prs)

Cls to centre edge, add 1 pr W, to
become passive pr 9 from outer edge 1
Tw 2 leaders, pin, edge st
Set aside extreme centre edge pr
DB:Pp (14 passive prs)

Note: There are now 8 prs set aside,
including outer edge 2 pr VDBb.

Cls leaders VDB back to outer edge 1
Pin C, edge st
Return leaders thro 2 prs only, leave
*Take 1st passive pr at centre edge
(MB/LB)
Cls this pr thro passives to outer
edge 1
Pin and edge st
Return thro 6 passive prs, leave
Note: Do not pull leader pr too
tightly, otherwise work will be pulled
too far away from centre pin; pulling
gently on the pr now nearest the
centre will control the size of hole.*

Repeat * to * 9 times more
Note: Join to section 3, flower, using
top sewings, T O & T B outer edge
1 pr VDBa.

After pin D, when returning for 9th
and final repeat:
Return leader pr thro all prs to centre
edge (see 1.58).
Hang 1 pr W, on temp pin above the
last centre edge pin, to be new leaders
Cls new leaders thro all passive prs,
from centre edge to pinned edge
section 3, flower rim (see 1.58)

After pin D:
From the centre edge to pinned edge
section 3, order is as foll:
MB
LB
MB

LB
MB
LB
W
LB
6 x W
****
W
LB
MB
LB
MB
DB:Pp
MB
DB:Pp
Pp
3 x VDB
Pp
VDB
Pp
VDB
Leaders 2 x W

After pin D (see 1.58):
Add 7 prs W to centre of braid,
indicated ******* in previous thread
order
Note: Include set aside prs from centre
edge when reached; Tw 2 leaders,
replace pin, Cls to section 3 or 4
(see 1.58).

At the same time, T O & T B prs
VDB
DB:Pp/MB
VDB/Pp
from the side of braid nearest
section 3
T O & T B pr MB/LB from the side of
braid nearest centre edge

After pin E:
T O & T B pr Pp/VDB from the side
of braid nearest section 4

After pin F (see 1.58):

Divide centre passives to make T.S. with 7th pr W, (from section 4 side of braid)

Start patt, Orchid 1

Follow instructions for Afternoon Dainty, version 1, section 4, petal (see 1.18)

After pin G (see 1.58):

T O & T B passive prs from each side of braid as foll:

Section 4	Centre edge
W	MB/LB
W	DB:Pp
MB/LB	VDB/Pp
	VDB/Pp
	VDB/Pp

Note: Outer edge 2 pr VDBb is included at pin A♯.

Outer edge 2
VDB/Pp
LB/W

After including outer edge 2 pr at pin A♯ (see 1.58 & 1.61), order is as foll:

Outer edge 2 pr, 2 x VDB

Leaders 2 x W

VDB

Pp

2 x DB:Pp

MB

LB

17 x W

LB

MB

DB:Pp

Pp

Section 4 edge VDB (16 prs)

After 3 patt repeats, make T.S.

Cont in Cls

After pin H (see 1.58), as braid narrows:

T O & T B prs from centre as foll:

8 x W

W/LB

LB/MB

MB/DB:Pp

DB:Pp

Pp

To finish, sew rem prs into section 4 (see 1.58)

T O & T B in a bunch

SECTION 4B, FLOWER

Follow instructions for section 4a, flower, using diagrams to correspond as foll:

Section 4a > section 4b

1.58 > 1.58

1.59 > 1.62

1.60 > 1.63

1.61 > 1.64

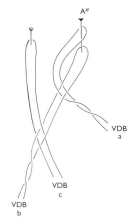

1.62 Morning Glory & Budding Glory section 4b, start

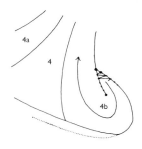

1.63 Morning Glory & Budding Glory section 4b, working direction

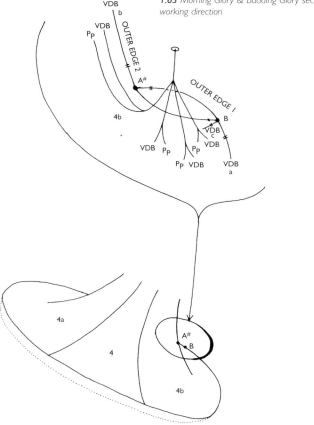

1.64 Morning Glory & Budding Glory section 4b, setting up prs and working pin A♯ to pin B

BUDDING GLORY
SECTION 1, STEM (SEE 1.46)

Follow instructions for Morning Glory, using colours to correspond as foll:

Morning Glory > Budding Glory

DG > DG

VDB > VDR

VDG > VDG

MG > MG

DB:Pp > VDR

SECTION 2, LEAF (SEE 1.3)

Follow instructions for Morning Glory, using colours to correspond as foll:

Morning Glory > Budding Glory

MG > MG

DG > DG

VDG > VDG

VDB > VDR

See also notes for Afternoon Dainties, versions 1 & 3, section 3, leaf

SECTION 3, FLOWER RIM (SEE 1.56)

Follow instructions for Morning Glory, using colours to correspond as foll:

Morning Glory > Budding Glory

DB:Pp > DP (VDR or F, see note)

W > C

LB > DC

MB > LP

Note: To work the inner pinned edge pr, use F instead of DB:Pp if choosing the red combination of colours and including the bud; use VDR instead of DB:Pp if choosing the red

combination of colours but not including bud in the design.

START pin A#:

Hang 3 prs in order as foll:

DC

F or VDR

DC (see 1.65)

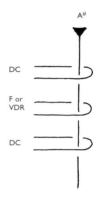

1.65 Budding Glory section 3, start pin A#

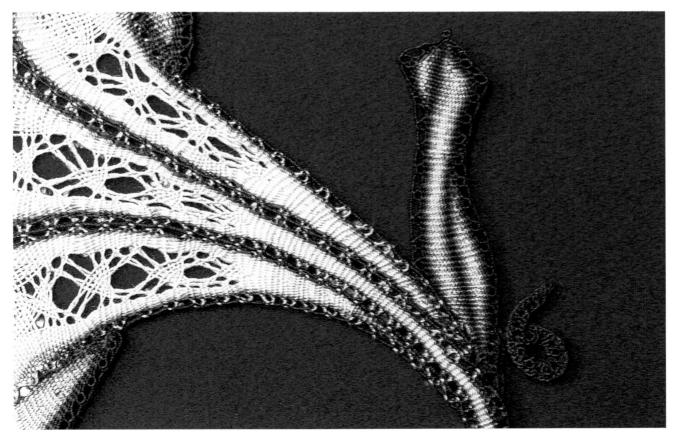

Budding Glory (detail)

SECTION 4, FLOWER (SEE 1.57)

Follow instructions for Morning Glory, using colours to correspond as foll:

Morning Glory > Budding Glory

W > C

LB > DC

MB > LP

DB:Pp > DP

VDB > VDR

Pp > F

VDG > VDG

SECTION 4A, FLOWER (SEE 1.58)

Follow instructions for Morning Glory, using colours to correspond as foll:

Morning Glory > Budding Glory

W > C

LB > DC

MB > LP

DB:Pp > DP

VDB > VDR

Pp > F

SECTION 4B, FLOWER (SEE 1.58)

Follow instructions for Morning Glory, using colours as given for Budding Glory, section 4a, flower

SECTION 5, BUD (SEE 1.66)

START at pin A# (one-colour point start):

Hang 2 prs VDR open around pin A# (see 1.67)

Work false picot: Tw 3, Cls prs tog

Tw 2 inner edge pr only

Hang 1 pr VDR leaders on temp pin

Cls leaders thro untwisted pr VDR

Tw 2 outer edge pr VDR

Hang 1 pr F, and 2 prs VDR on temp pin, in single thread order as foll:

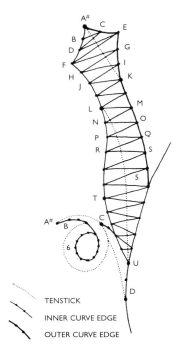

1.66 Budding Glory sections 5 & 6, pin reference plan

TENSTICK

INNER CURVE EDGE

OUTER CURVE EDGE

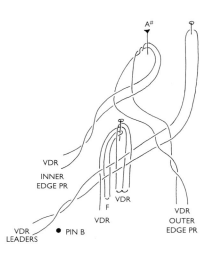

1.67 Budding Glory section 5, one-colour point start

VDR

VDR

VDR

F

F

VDR (see 1.67)

Cls leaders VDR thro 3 prs on temp

pin

Tw 2 leaders,

Pin B, edge st with inner edge pr VDR (6 prs)

Pin B to pin C:

Add 2 prs VDR

3 prs F to give order as foll:

Inner edge pr 2 x VDR

3 x VDR

4 x F

3 x *VDR*

4 x F

2 x VDR

Outer edge pr 2 x VDR

Leaders 2 x VDR (11 prs)

Note: Threads *VDR* are to follow the dotted line A# to K (see 1.66).

Pin C to pin D:

Add 3 prs DP to give order as foll:

Inner edge pr 2 x VDR

3 x VDR

2 x F

4 x DP

2 x F

3 x *VDR*

2 x F

2 x DP

2 x F

2 x VDR

Outer edge pr 2 x VDR

Leaders 2 x VDR (14 prs)

Pin D to pin E:

Add 1 pr DP

2 prs LP

1 pr C to give order as foll:

Inner edge pr 2 x VDR

3 x VDR

2 x F

2 x DP

LP

2 x DP

LP

2 x DP

2 x F

3 x *VDR*

2 x F

DP

LP

2 x C

LP

DP

2 x F

2 x VDR

Outer edge pr 2 x VDR

Leaders 2 x VDR (18 prs)

Pin E to pin F:

Add 2 prs LP to give order as foll:

Inner edge pr 2 x VDR

3 x VDR

2 x F

2 x DP

LP

DP

4 x LP

DP

LP

2 x DP

2 x F

3 x *VDR*

2 x F

DP

LP

2 x C

LP

DP

2 x F

2 x VDR

Outer edge pr 2 x VDR

Leaders 2 x VDR (20 prs)

Note: After pin E, tie ½ knot with leaders between 1st passive pr VDR and 2nd passive pr F, from outer edge.

Pin F to pin G:

Add 1 pr C to give order as foll:

Inner edge pr 2 x VDR

3 x VDR

2 x F

2 x DP

LP

DP

2 x LP

2 x C

2 x LP

DP

LP

2 x DP

2 x F

3 x *VDR*

2 x F

DP

LP

2 x C

LP

DP

2 x F

2 x VDR

Outer edge pr 2 x VDR

Leaders 2 x VDR

Note: After pin F, tie ½ knot with leaders between 1st passive pr VDR and 2nd passive pr VDR/F from inner edge. After pin G, T O & T B 4th passive pr C from outer edge (20 prs).

After pin G:

Order is as foll:

Inner edge pr 2 x VDR

3 x VDR

2 x F

2 x DP

LP

DP

2 x LP

2 x C

2 x LP

DP

LP

2 x DP

2 x F

3 x *VDR*

2 x F

DP

2 x LP

DP

2 x F

2 x VDR

Outer edge pr 2 x VDR

Leaders 2 x VDR

Note: After pin H, T O & T B passives 2 & 3, VDR/F and passives 6 & 7, 2 x LP from outer edge (18 prs).

After pin H:

Order is as foll:

Inner edge pr 2 x VDR

3 x VDR

2 x F

2 x DP

LP

DP

2 x LP

2 x C

2 x LP

DP

LP

2 x DP

2 x F

3 x *VDR*

2 x F

2 x DP

F

VDR

Outer edge pr 2 x VDR

Leaders 2 x VDR

Note: After pin I, T O & T B 2nd passive pr DP, and passives 6 & 7, F/VDR (passive VDR is from *VDR* group) from outer edge. After pin J, T O & T B passives 2 & 3, F from outer edge (15 prs).

After pin L:

Add 1 pr VDR to become 2nd passive pr from inner edge, order is as foll:

Inner edge pr 2 x VDR

2 x VDR

3 x *VDR*

2 x F

2 x DP

LP

DP

2 x LP

2 x C

2 x LP

DP

LP

2 x DP

2 x F

3 x VDR

Outer edge pr 2 x VDR

Leaders 2 x VDR

Note: After pin L, T O & T B 4th passive pr DP/LP and 9th passive pr DP/LP from outer edge. Threads *VDR* are to follow dotted line from pin L to pin U at finish (14 prs).

After pin M:
Add 1 pr F

After pin N:
Add 1 pr F

After pin O:
Add 1 pr DP

After pin P:
Add 1 pr DP

After pin Q:
Add 1 pr LP

After pin R:
Add 1 pr LP

After pin S:
Add 1 pr C, to give order as foll:
Inner edge pr 2 x VDR

2 x VDR

2 x F

2 x DP

2 x LP

2 x C

2 x LP

2 x DP

2 x F

3 x *VDR*

2 x F

2 x DP

2 x LP

2 x C

2 x LP

2 x DP

2 x F

3 x VDR

Outer edge pr 2 x VDR

Leaders 2 x VDR (21 prs)

Note: Join section 5 to section 4b using top sewings, T O & T B outer edge pr VDR.

After pin T, when braid narrows:
T O & T B at each row:
2 prs C from centre and 1 pr VDR from outer edge
2 prs LP from centre and 1 pr VDR/F from outer edge
2 prs LP from centre and 1 pr VDR/F from outer edge
1 pr DP from centre and 1 pr DP from outer edge
1 pr DP from centre and 1 pr DP/F from outer edge
1 pr F from centre and 1 pr F/VDR from outer edge
1 pr F from centre and 1 pr VDR from outer edge

After pin U, to finish:
T O & T B rem prs in a bunch, and secure to work with previously T B prs

SECTION 6, TENDRIL (SEE 1.66)

Note: Pinned edge of Tenstick starts on the inner curve, but at the crossing of the tendril the pinned edge changes to the outer curve.
START at pin A# (Tenstick colour point start, see 1.68):

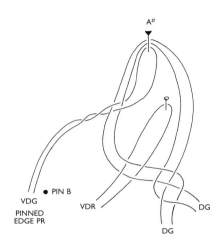

1.68 Budding Glory section 6, Tenstick colour point start

Hang 2 prs DG and 1 pr VDG open around pin A#
Cls pr VDG thro pr DG
Tw 2 pr DG, pinned edge pr
Note: The 2 prs DG are the leader prs that will work the Tenstick.
Hang 1 pr VDR on temp pin
Cls pr DG thro pr VDR
Work smooth Tenstick edge st (X T X T X) with both prs DG
Work pr DG back to pinned edge, Tw 2
Pin B & edge st with pr VDG (4 prs)
Cont in Tenstick
When the Tenstick braid crosses, join with a top sewing

Before working pin C:
Change the pinned edge of the Tenstick thus:

Follow instructions given for Morning Glory, section 1, stem, at pin T1 (see 1.54)

Join tendril to section 5, bud, with top sewings

T O & T B pinned edge pr

At pin D, to finish:

T O & T B rem prs in a bunch

OPTION

Budding Glory may be worked using the blue combination of threads; if so, complete section 5, bud, and section 6, tendril, in colours to correspond as foll:

Budding Glory > Morning Glory

Bud VDR > VDB

F > Pp

DP > DB:Pp

LP > MB

C > W

Tendril VDG > VDG

DG > DG

VDR > VDB

Second Thoughts, with a rolled edge. Pipers Silks 80/3 and 90/3

PAINTING WITH THREADS

Chapter 2

The following series of patterns mainly concentrates on the opportunity to explore the ideas and practise some of the colour techniques necessary to work Sea Swirl and On Reflection.

The working instructions are not quite as explicit as those given in the previous chapter, but are still highly detailed. Where an obvious design link runs through several patterns, the most detailed instructions will appear with the first in the series; subsequent patterns will cover variations and design differences in detail.

CROCUS LEAVES

This is a deceptively simple design emphasizing the importance of open spaces in lacemaking. It is worked in cloth stitch and Tenstick throughout, with just the addition of cloth stitch and twist to emphasize the leaf vein.

The illusion of the leaves twisting and turning in sunlight and shade is created by the blending of different shades (yellow/greens and blue/greens) and tones (dark and light), which add depth to this piece. In all, seven

different types of green have been used. Some of the leaves incorporate rolled (Withof) edges. These are optional, but their addition encourages the illusion of depth.

Pricking Size: See 2.1
100%: Pipers Silks
80/3 Spun silk
*90/3 Gloss silk

Thread: Pipers Silks (see Pricking notes) 80/3 and *90/3 are shown in the worked sample. These thread types are interchangeable. It is these threads that are described in the instructions, their names given in an abbreviated form. Should any other threads be substituted, the pricking scale may have to be changed and the finished piece will not look exactly the same.

Colours: Apple Green APP
Pea Green PEA
Pastel Green PAS

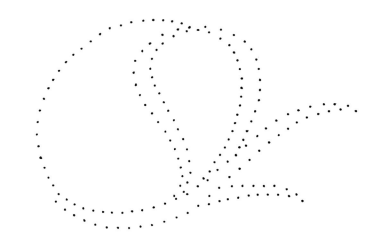

2.1 Crocus Leaves, pricking

Dark Green D.GR

Malachite Green MAL

*Bottle Green *BOT

Dark Tartan D.TAR

Note: * denotes 90/3 Gloss silk;
all other threads are 80/3 Spun silk.

Techniques: No (colour) change edge
   stitch

One-colour point start

False picot

Colour shading in narrow braid

Colour shading in Tenstick

Changing braid to Tenstick

Changing Tenstick leader prs

Changing/shading prs near Tenstick
   smooth edge

Roll (Withof)

Top sewings

Adding and discarding prs to edge of
   narrow braid

Narrow-angle start

Stitches and Braids: Cloth stitch

Tenstick

Cloth stitch & twist

To Work: Work each section
numerically as shown in 2.2. No
(colour) change edge st is used
throughout. Top sewings are used
throughout. Colours/threads are
shown singly in thread order listings,
unless otherwise indicated.

SECTION 1 (SEE 2.2)

START at pin A# (one-colour point
start, see 1.13):

Hang 2 prs *BOT open around pin
A#, Tw 3

On temp pins, add 1 pr leaders *BOT
and 2 prs *BOT passives, work to
pin B

Cont in Cls, adding 5 prs to centre of
braid, as foll:

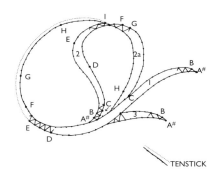

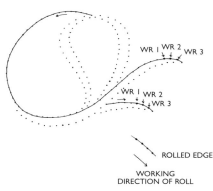

2.2 *Crocus Leaves, pin reference plan and
working order*

2.3 *Crocus Leaves, edges to be rolled*

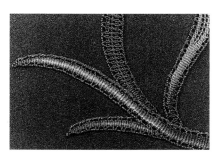

Crocus leaves (detail). Pointed start and rolled edges

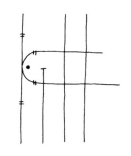

2.4 *Crocus Leaves, adding prs to edge of braid*

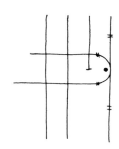

2.5 *Crocus Leaves, discarding prs from edge of braid*

1 pr MAL

1 pr D.GR

1 pr APP

1 pr APP

1 pr PEA (10 prs)

After pin C:

Add 1 pr MAL to become passives
3 & 4 from left edge

T O & T B passives 3 & 4 from right
edge

Add 1 pr *BOT to become passives
3 & 4 from left edge

T O & T B passives 3 & 4 from right
edge

Add 1 pr D.TAR to become passives
1 & 2 from left edge, after pin has
been placed

Note: When passive prs must be
added to the edge of a braid,
particularly a narrow braid, the
slightly jagged edge is more easily

disguised if the pair is added after the
pin has been placed and the edge st
worked, and also if the braid is tightly
packed. Likewise, when discarding a
passive pr at the edge of a braid, pin
& edge st first (see 2.4, 2.5).

Add 1 pr D.TAR to become passives
3 & 4 from left edge

T O & T B passives 3 & 4 from right
edge

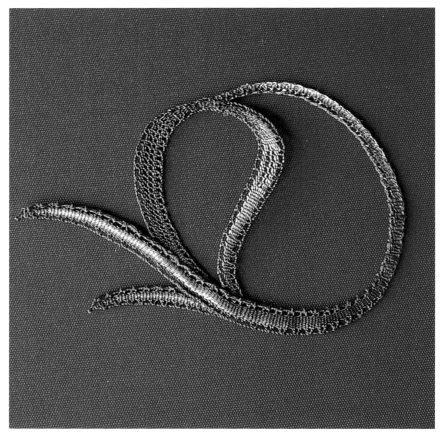

Crocus Leaves. Pipers Silks 80/3 and 90/3

Add 1 pr D.TAR to become passives
3 & 4 from left edge
T O & T B passives 3 & 4 from right
edge
Add 1 pr D.TAR to become passives
3 & 4 from left edge
T O & T B passives 3 & 4 from right
edge (11 prs)

After pin D, where braid narrows:
*T O & T B 1 pr passives 3 & 4 from
right side*
Rep * to * twice more (8 prs)

At pin E:
Change to Tenstick (see 1.49) keeping
pinned edge on the left
Note: After a few pins have been
worked, remove pin D; this will give a
smoother edge.

After pin F:
Start introducing lighter prs from the
smooth edge at the right:
D.TAR
*BOT
MAL
PAS
PEA
and removing darker prs from the
pinned edge on the left
This is achieved in Tenstick by
changing both the leading prs and
some of the passives from the smooth
edge side thus:
Note: Extreme care must be taken
when changing prs in Tenstick, to
maintain even tension.
< Changing both the leading prs in
Tenstick:
Work to pinned edge, pin, edge st

Cls thro 1st passive pr
Hang new lighter pr on temp pin
Cls thro new pr
T O & T B old leaders
Cont with new pr as new leaders
(see 2.6)
Work to smooth edge, make usual
smooth edge T.S. (X T X T X)
Note: It will be seen that the new
leaders have been split.
Cont with leaders, one thread light
and one thread dark
Work to the next smooth edge
(see 2.7)
Note: At this smooth edge st, give an
extra twist (X T X T T X) (see 2.8),
so that the split leader pr is rearranged
to become the darker pr, thus enabling
this second darker leader pr to be
changed to a lighter pr as before (see
2.6) after the next pin has been
worked.
In order to speed up the shading in
the Tenstick from darker to lighter
threads, lighter passives may be
introduced near the smooth edge as
foll (see 2.9):
Add 1 pr lighter thread, in this case
MAL, to hang inside smooth edge pr
Work leaders back from pinned edge,
thro added pr and make T.S. at
smooth edge
T O & T B 1 pr, a darker thread, in
this case D.TAR, from left edge
(8 prs) >
Cont in Tenstick

After pin G (while cont to lighten
threads on smooth edge):
T O & T B 2 prs from left edge to
allow Tenstick to reduce (6 prs)

After pin H:
Commence shading light back to
dark, as before, by changing leader prs

and passive prs as foll:

PEA

PAS

MAL

*BOT

D.TAR (see 2.6, 2.7, 2.8, 2.9)

T O & T B 1 passive pr (5 prs)

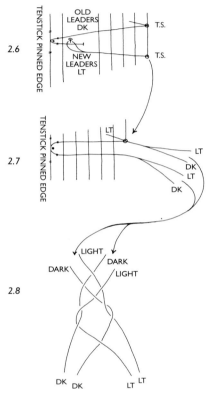

2.6 Crocus Leaves, introducing new leaders to Tenstick

2.7 Crocus Leaves, changing part of the leader pr at the smooth edge in Tenstick

2.8 Crocus Leaves, detail of T.S. variation at smooth edge, to change colours

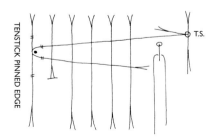

2.9 Crocus Leaves, introducing passive pr near smooth edge in Tenstick

At pin I:

Cls leaders thro all 3 rem passives

Tie ½ knot with leaders

Place 2 right side passive prs and leader pr aside and make secure

Note: These prs will be needed later and joined to section 2a.

Use the rem 2 prs (edge pr & 1 passive pr) to roll back

Note: Turn work around thro 180 degrees (see 2.3).

To roll:

Untwist the edge pr, use it to tie ½ knot with passive pr

Proceed to make the rolled edge thus:

Remove 1st pin

Insert very fine 0.4mm crochet hook into work under the edge prs, as if making a side sewing, under all threads to be included in roll (see 2.10)

< Pull the rolling thread thro, under the roll threads and edge pr to make a loop

Pass the end of the rolling thread bobbin thro the loop which has been created, enclosing the roll threads and edge pr (see 2.11)

Pull up the rolling thread gently across the work to tighten around the enclosed threads

Replace pin

Cont to roll in the direction indicated (2.11) >

At pin WR 1:

T B 1 thread from roll

At pin WR 2:

T B 1 thread from roll

At pin WR 3, to finish roll (see 2.12):

Make side sewing to attach roll, then make top sewing into the bar of the same pinhole

T O & T B both threads

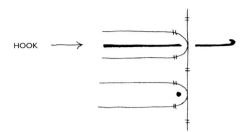

2.10 Crocus Leaves, direction of hook insertion for (Withof) roll

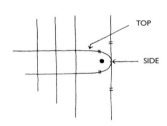

2.11 Crocus Leaves, working (Withof) roll

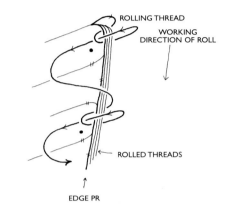

2.12 Crocus Leaves, finishing (Withof) roll

SECTION 2 (SEE 2.2)

START at pin A#:

Narrow-angle start, thus:

Using a top sewing, hang on 1 pr *BOT (right edge pr)

Tw 2, do not tighten loop yet (see 2.13)

Thread 1 pr *BOT (left edge pr) and 1 pr *BOT (leaders) thro loop of right edge pr

Pull gently right edge pr to tighten loop

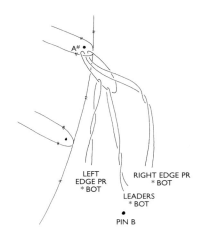

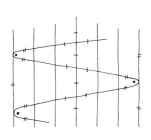

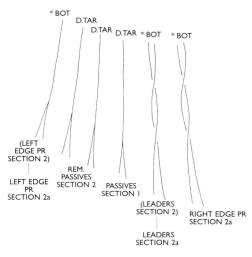

2.13 Crocus Leaves, narrow-angle start

2.14 Crocus Leaves, pattern in centre of braid, Cls & Tw with 3rd passive pr

2.15 Crocus Leaves, Section 2a, thread order after joining section 2 to section 1 at pin 1

Tw 2 left edge pr and leaders

At pin B:

Edge st with leaders and right edge pr
Cont in Cls, adding 2 prs D.TAR on
next row, then 1 pr D.Tar on the
following row, to the centre of the
braid (6 prs)

After pin C, each row (see 2.4 & 2.5):
Add 1 pr *BOT to left edge
Add 1 pr MAL to left edge
Add 1 pr MAL to left edge
T O & T B 1 pr D.TAR from right
edge
Add 2 prs D.GR to left edge
T O & T B 1 pr D.TAR from right
edge
Add 2 prs APP to left edge
T O & T B 1 pr D.TAR from right
edge
Add 1 pr APP to left edge
T O & T B 1 pr *BOT from right
edge
Add 1 pr APP to left edge
T O & T B 1 pr MAL from right edge
Add 1 pr APP to left edge
T O & T B 1 pr MAL from right edge
(10 prs)

After pin D:
Tw 1 the 3rd passive pr from left edge
Cls leaders thro 2 passive prs, Tw 1

leaders
Cls & Tw with 3rd passive pr
(see 2.14)
T O & T B 1 pr D.GR from right edge
(9 prs)
Cont with braid, working Cls & Tw
with 3rd passive pr
T O & T B 1 pr D.GR from right edge
(8 prs)

After pin E:
Add 1 pr each side of braid, using a
darker shade of green at every row
As braid narrows, cont in Cls
throughout
T O & T B prs from centre of braid,
leaving 5 prs of the darkest shades
remaining

At pin I, section 1:
Using top sewings, join section 2 to
section 1
T O & T B right edge pr, section 2
T O & T B lightest pr from section 1,
and secure
Place darkest pr from section 1
alongside prs from section 2, to be
passives for section 2a
Use *BOT pr from section 1 as new
right edge pr for section 2a
Take *BOT leaders from section 2,
having made top sewing into pin I, as
new leaders for section 2a, Tw 2
(see 2.15)

SECTION 2A (SEE 2.2)

After pin F:
Add lighter prs to centre of braid, to
give order as foll:
Left edge pr 2 x *BOT
3 x D.TAR
4 x *BOT
3 x D.TAR
Right edge pr 2 x *BOT
Leaders 2 x *BOT (8 prs)

After pin G:
Cls & Tw with central pr, as in
section 2 (see 2.14)

After pin H:
Cont in Cls, and using top sewings,
join section 2a to section 1
T O & T B prs as braid narrows

SECTION 3 (SEE 2.2)

START at pin A#:
Hang 2 prs *BOT open around pin
A#, Tw 3 (one-colour point start,
see 1.13)
On temp pins, add 1pr *BOT leaders
and 2 prs *BOT passives,
work to pin B
Add prs to centre of braid as foll:
1 pr *BOT
1 pr MAL

1 pr MAL
1 pr PAS (9 prs)
Cont in Cls

At pin C:
Join section 3 to section 1 with top sewings
T O & T B left edge pr and 1st left edge passive pr
Note: Do not cut off these two prs *BOT, they will be used to roll back later.
Cont with rem prs, joining with top sewings to section 1, T O & T B prs to decrease as the braid reaches the point
T O & T B rem prs in a bunch to finish
Return to the 2 prs left at pin C to roll back
Follow instructions given after pin I, section 1 (see 2.10, 2.11, 2.12)
To finish:
At pin WR 1, T B 1 thread from roll
At pin WR 2, T B 1 thread from roll
At pin WR 3, T B 1 thread from roll

CROCUS

Crocus, using exactly the same pricking as Crocus Leaves, demonstrates how a design can be radically changed simply by placing a different emphasis on open space.

In referring to the linear illustration, 2.16, it is possible to imagine several different ways of working this design in colour, depending upon those areas which are to be considered solid and worked in lace, and those which are to be left open. Some suggestions have included a dewdrop dripping from leaves, a snail or a butterfly.

It is a design that easily lends itself to experimentation. However, to experiment further it is essential to

Crocus leaves (detail). Joining sections with top sewings

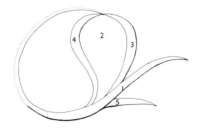

2.16 Crocus, working order

make colour studies first, on tracing or layout paper, which can then be placed over the pricking to ensure that the idea is workable. Choice of braid or lace textures can be planned in the same way.

There are two colour versions of Crocus: version 1 (lilac) and version 2 (primrose) – see Colour notes. Both versions are worked identically, using some of the techniques from earlier patterns and Crocus Leaves. The main difference in this piece is that the Milanese braid chosen is a variation of Lattice 3, and is shaped to fit the design.

By using the variation and plotting the colours carefully, it can be seen that both the crocus petal shapes and the three-dimensional shape of the flower are enhanced, creating shapes within shapes.

Pricking Size: See 2.1
100%: Pipers Silks
80/3 Spun silk
*90/3 Gloss silk
**300 Semi-gloss silk (white)

Thread: Pipers Silks (see Pricking notes), 80/3, *90/3 and **300 Semi-gloss (white) are shown in the sample. These thread types are interchangeable; however, do not mix *90/3 white with **Semi-gloss white in the same piece. See also Thread notes for Crocus Leaves.

Colours: Version 1 > version 2
*Seafoam S.F. > *Seafoam S.F.
Pastel PAS > Pastel PAS
Pea PEA > Pea PEA
*Mint *MIN > Pale Lime P.LI
**White **W > **White **W
*Sky *SKY > Ecru EC
*Hyacinth *HY > *Ivory *IV
*Delft *DEL > Cream CR
*Pansy *PAN > *Butter *BUT
Note: ** denotes 300 Semi-gloss silk and * denotes 90/3 Gloss silk; all other threads are 80/3 Spun silk.

Techniques: No (colour) change edge
    stitch
One-colour point start
False picot

Colour shading in narrow braid

Changing braid to Tenstick

Use of magic threads

Working a shaped area of Milanese
  braid pattern

Top sewings

Narrow-angle start

Stitches and Braids: Cloth stitch

Lattice 3 (variation)

Tenstick

To Work: Work each section
numerically as shown in 2.16. No
(colour) change edge st is used
throughout. Top sewings are used
throughout. Colours/threads are
shown singly in thread order listings,
unless otherwise indicated.

SECTION 1 (SEE 2.17)

* START at pin A# (one-colour point
start, see 1.13):

Hang 2 prs *S.F. open around pin A#,
Tw 3

On temp pins, add 1 pr leaders *S.F.
and 2 prs *S.F. passives, work to pin B

Cont in Cls, adding 5 prs to braid, to
give order L to R as foll:

Left edge pr (lighter side of leaf)

2 x *S.F.

1 x *MIN

2 x **W

1 x *MIN

2 x *PEA

2 x PAS

2 x *S.F.

2 x PAS

2 x *S.F.

Right edge pr (darker side of leaf)

2 x *S.F.

Leaders 2 x *S.F. (10 prs)

Cont in Cls

**

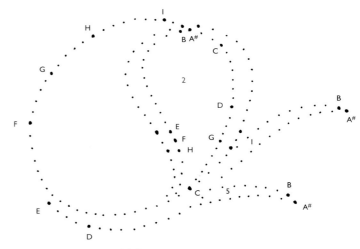

2.17 Crocus, pin reference plan, sections 1, 2 & 5

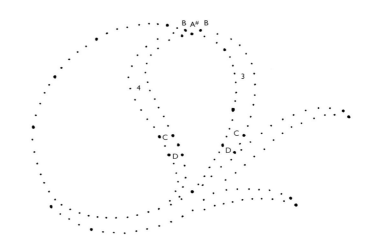

2.18 Crocus, pin reference plan, sections 3 & 4

After pin C:

Add 1 pr **W to become passives
3 & 4 from left edge (11 prs)

After pin D:

T O & T B 4 prs as foll:

1 pr **W

1 pr **W

1 pr PEA/MIN

1 pr PEA/MIN (7 prs)

After pin E:

Secure threads and leave to finish
after working sections 2, 3 & 4

SECTION 2

START at pin A# (one-colour point
start, see 1.13):

Hang 2 prs *PAN open around pin
A#, Tw 5

Use a magic thread, before Cls prs tog
(see 2.19)

Note: A magic thread can be used to
facilitate sewings, especially when a
pinhole will need to be used several
times, or when there will not be much
space to make the sewing, or
whenever exceptional strain may be
placed on the existing work.

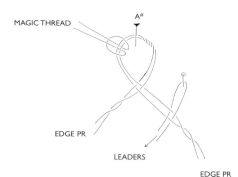

MAGIC THREAD

A#

EDGE PR

LEADERS

EDGE PR

2.19 Crocus, using a magic thread

< To use a magic thread (see 2.19):
Place a doubled thread (of a
contrasting colour) under the work
where the sewing will be made
Thread loose ends thro loop to secure,
leave until sewing is to be made
To make a sewing using a magic
thread:
Unthread loose ends from loop
Thread one bobbin from the pr to be
sewn in thro the loop
Pull gently on the loose ends of the
magic thread until the looped thread
from the bobbin is through
Place the other bobbin from the pr
thro its partner's loop to make the
sewing
Remove magic thread
To replace a magic thread so the
pinhole can be used again:
When threading the first bobbin thro
the loop of the original magic thread,
at the same time hang in another
magic thread
When the original magic thread is
pulled through, along with the looped
thread from the bobbin to make the
sewing, so will the loop from the
second magic thread
Place loose ends thro loop as before >
On temp pin, add 1 pr leaders *SKY
On another temp pin hang 4 prs open
to give order as foll:

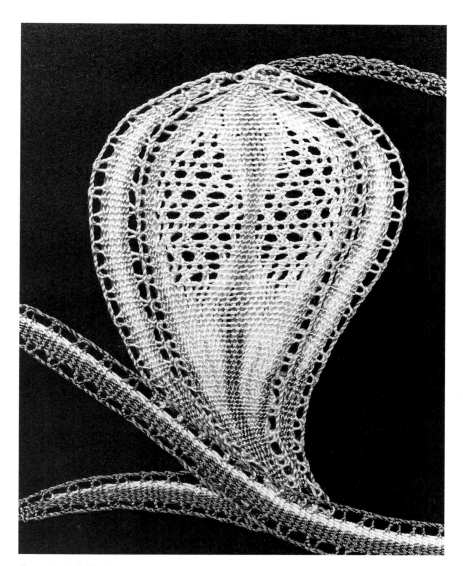

Crocus. Version 2 (detail)

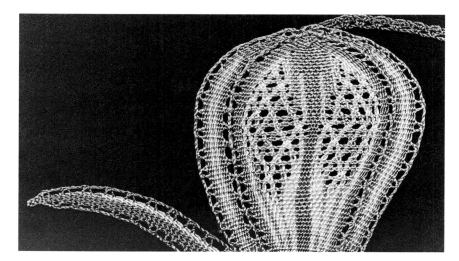

Crocus, version 1 (detail). Lattice 3, variation

*DEL, *PAN, *DEL, 2 x *PAN,
*DEL, *PAN, *DEL (7 prs)
Cls leaders thro these 4 prs to pin B
Pin B to pin C:
On another temp pin hang 4 prs open
to give order as foll:
*HY, *SKY, *HY, 2 x *DEL, *HY,
*SKY, *HY (11 prs)
On each of the next 4 rows, add prs as
indicated:
Add 1 pr *PAN (to centre)
and 2 prs *SKY

Add 2 prs *SKY
and 2 prs **W

Add 2 prs **W
and 2 prs **W

Add 2 prs **W
and 2 prs **W (26 prs)

Order is now:
Edge pr 2 x *PAN
*DEL
*PAN
*DEL
*PAN
*HY
2 x *SKY
10 x **W
3 x *SKY
****
*HY
*DEL
2 x *PAN
*DEL
*HY
****
3 x *SKY
10 x **W
2 x *SKY
*HY
*PAN
*DEL

*PAN
*DEL
Edge pr 2 x *PAN
Leaders 2 x *SKY (26 prs)

After pin C:
Add 1 pr **W at each *******
position indicated in the previous
thread list (28 prs)
Start patt Lattice 3, variation
(see 2.20)
Note: Variation of Lattice 3 is worked
using 2 passive prs per Cls set, Tw 1
between prs (see 2.20). Section 2 is
composed of two parts, each the
mirror image of the other, either side
of the central passive pr 2 x *PAN
(see 2.21).
Patt thus:
Cls tog passive prs 6 & 7 from both
sides of section 2
After edge st at pin C,
Cls leaders thro 5 passive prs, Tw 1
leaders

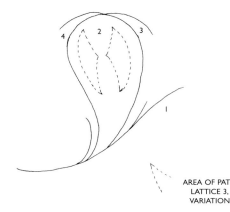

*2.21 Crocus, section 2, shaped area of Lattice 3
variation*

Cls leaders thro 1 pr, Tw 1 leaders
Rep * to * once more
Cont in Cls until prs 6 & 7
(previously Cls tog) are reached
Tw 1 leaders
Rep * to * twice, Cls to end of row
Cont as in patt diagram 2.20

After pin D:
Cont in Cls, order is as foll:

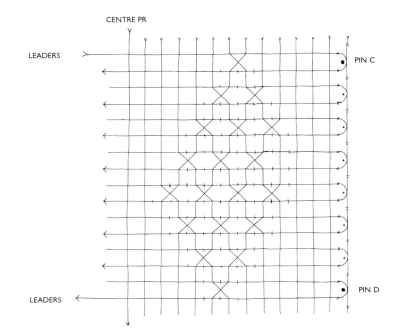

2.20 Crocus, section 2, working diagram of Lattice 3 variation, for shaped area of petal

Edge pr 2 x *PAN
*DEL
*PAN
*DEL
*PAN
*HY
*SKY
3 x **W
3 x *SKY
4 x **W
*SKY
5 x **W
*HY
*DEL
2 x *PAN
*DEL
*HY
5 x **W
*SKY
4 x **W
3 x *SKY
3 x **W
*SKY
*HY
*PAN
*DEL
*PAN
*DEL
Edge pr 2 x *PAN
Leaders 2 x *SKY (28 prs)

After pin E:
Add 2 prs *S.F., 1 pr either side of
centre pr *PAN (30 prs)

After pin F:
Add 2 prs *MIN, to both sides of
petal, to become passives 17 & 18
from the edges (32 prs)

After pin G:
As work begins to narrow T O & T B
prs evenly, lightest shades first,
allowing work to become striped

After pin H:
Add 2 prs *S.F., to both sides of petal,
to become passives 3 & 4 from the
edges
Work 2 blind pins
To finish, join to section 1 with top
sewings

SECTION 3 (SEE 2.18)

Start at pin A# (narrow-angle start,
see 2.13):
Into pin A#, using the magic thread,
hang on 1 pr *PAN to be edge pr
Thread 1 pr *SKY (leaders) and 1 pr
*PAN (passives) thro loop of edge pr
Cls leaders *SKY thro passive pr
*PAN to pin B (3 prs)
Cont in Cls, joining section 3 to
section 2 with top sewings, and adding
prs to centre of braid as foll:
1 pr *DEL
1 pr *PAN
1 pr *HY
1 pr *SKY
1 pr **W
1 pr **W
1 pr *SKY (10 prs)

After pin C:
T O & T B 2 prs **W/*SKY, keeping
the central pr *SKY intact (indicating
a vein in the petal) (8 prs)

After pin D:
Add 2 prs *S.F. to become passives
3 & 4 from both edges
T O & T B 2 prs **W/*HY (8 prs)
As braid narrows, cont T O & T B
prs, lightest shades first
To finish, join to sections 1 & 2 with
top sewings

SECTION 4 (SEE 2.18)

Complete to match section 3.

RETURN to section 1 (7 prs)
Change from braid to Tenstick
(see 1.49)
After a few pins have been worked,
for a smoother edge, remove pin E.

After pin F:
*T O & T B 2nd pr passives from
pinned edge*

After pins G & H:
Rep * to * (4 prs)

After pin I:
T O & T B 1st passive pr from pinned
edge (3 prs)
T O & T B central pr
To finish, join to section 4 with top
sewings at pin B

SECTION 5 (SEE 2.17)

(One-colour point start, see 1.13)
Follow instructions given for section
1, from * to **
To finish, join to section 1 with top
sewings

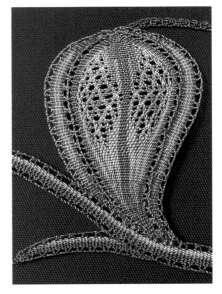

Crocus, version I (detail).

FISHTAILS

The fluid and circular motion created by the design of Fishtails is emphasized by there being only one start and finish. There is only one section to be worked in this piece.

Starting at the head of the fish, the work divides into two parts. One part of the body is completed, whereupon some of the threads are used for the roll, then the second part is worked. Note: It must be remembered that the roll needs to be attached to the part of the work that will appear to the forefront of the design. The same consideration is made when joining sections with top sewings.

When work recommences the braid has a complete colour change. This is to give the illusion of the fish twisting over (see bud, Budding Glory) and creating movement within the design.

The split in the fishtail reveals a fish shape which is repeated by yet another fish lurking in the depths of the water (see also Sea Swirl).

As can be seen, the unworked areas form an important and essential part of the design, as was previously mentioned in Crocus Leaves and Crocus.

Dewdrops and Ribbon were the braids used for the body of the fish, and were chosen to indicate the effect of light playing on fish scales under the water.

The braid choice allowing for extensive movement of threads has already been explored in earlier pieces. When choosing the braids for a design, the scale of the pattern shapes within the braid and the linking of braids with related patterns are as important as other considerations. This is illustrated in Fishtails.

Pricking Size: See 2.22
100%: Pipers Silks
80/3 Spun silks
*90/3 Gloss silks
**300 Semi-gloss silk (white)

Thread: Pipers Silks (see Pricking notes) 80/3, *90/3 and **300 Semi-gloss (white) are shown in the sample. See Thread notes for Crocus Leaves and Crocus.

Colours: *Olive *OLI
*Helio *HEL
*Mauve *MAU
*Pigeon *PIG
*Silver *SIL
Flesh FL
**White **W

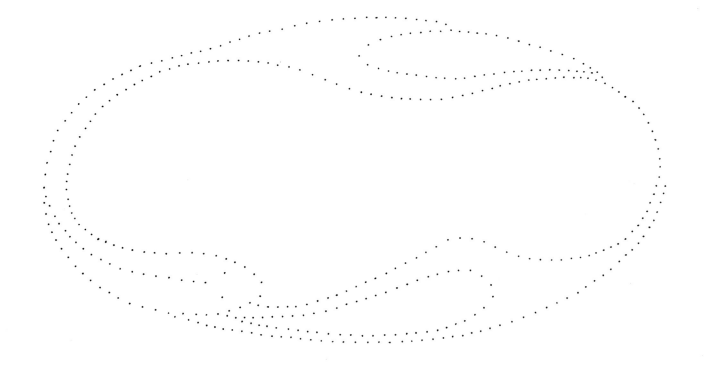

2.22 Fishtails, pricking

*Mint *MIN
*Sky *SKY
Pea PEA
*Seafoam *S.F.
*Hyacinth *HY
*Delft *DEL
Olive OL
*Pansy *PAN
Purple PUR
Apple APP
Note: ** denotes 300 Semi-gloss silk and * denotes 90/3 Gloss silk; all other threads are 80/3 Spun silk.

Techniques: No (colour) change edge stitch
Two-colour round start
Holes (eyes), retaining colours
Splitting braids (4 variations)
Turning stitch
Locking stitch
Changing passive prs in pattern

Changing leaders
Colour change/shading in braid, to introduce a different colour scheme, changing leaders and passives
Roll (Withof)
Changing thread colour within (Withof) roll, by adding and discarding single threads
Joining braid to rolled edge (top sewing)
Blind pin
Changing leaders, by making top sewing
Changing edge pr with passive pr
Working a shaped area of Milanese braid pattern
Changing leaders with passive pr
Changing to Tenstick
Joining two braids together
Changing Tenstick to pinned edge
Supported T.S. smooth edge
Top sewings

Stitches and Braids: Cloth stitch
Dewdrops
Ribbon
Lattice 3 (variation, see Crocus)
Cloth stitch & twist
Tenstick
½ stitch Tenstick

To Work: There is only one section. No (colour) change edge st is used throughout. Top sewings are used throughout. Colours/threads are shown singly in thread order listings, unless otherwise indicated.

SECTION 1 (SEE 2.23 & 2.24)
START at pin A# (two-colour round start):
Hang side by side on pin A#, 1 pr *OLI and 1 pr *HEL (see 2.25)
Cls both prs tog

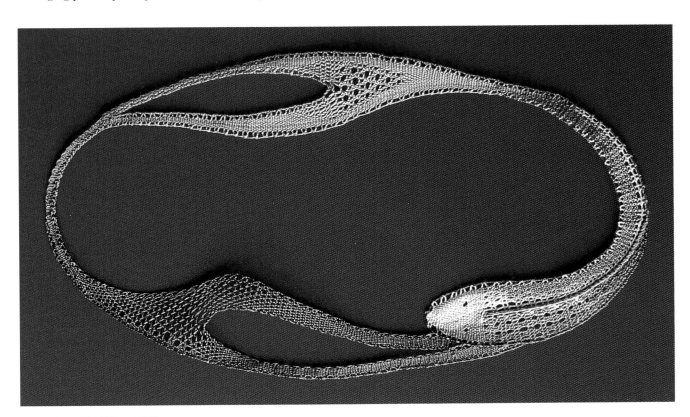

Fishtails. Pipers Silks 80/3 and 90/3

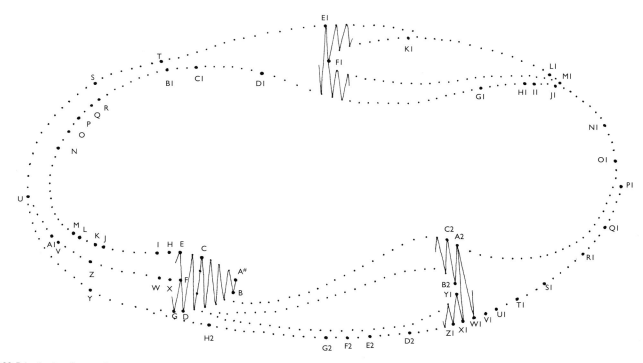

2.23 Fishtails, pin reference plan

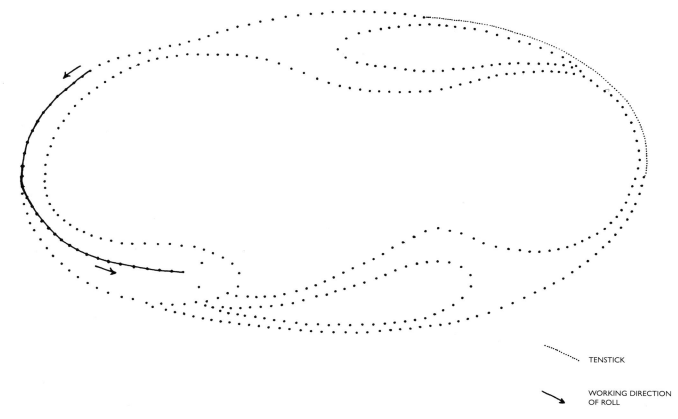

TENSTICK

WORKING DIRECTION
OF ROLL

2.24 Fishtails, rolled work and Tenstick section

60

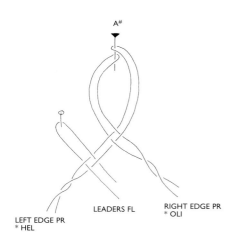

2 x **W
FL
2 x **W
4 x FL
*SIL
FL
*SIL
2 x *MIN
2 x *SKY
2 x *MIN
2 x PEA
2 x *S.F.
2 x *HY
*PIG
*DEL
*PIG
*DEL
Right edge pr 2 x *OLI
Leaders 2 x FL (25 prs)

2.25 Fishtails, two-colour round start

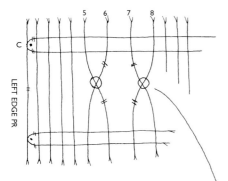

2.26 Fishtails, working small holes and retaining colours

Tw 2 right edge pr *OLI
On temp pin, hang 1 pr FL, leaders
Cls leaders thro untwisted pr *HEL
Tw 2 left edge pr *HEL
Cls across to pin B, adding 5 prs
Cont in Cls to pin C, adding a further
17 prs, to give order at pin C as foll:
Left edge pr 2 x *HEL
*MAU
*PIG
*MAU
*PIG
3 x *SIL
FL
*SIL
4 x FL
2 x **W
FL

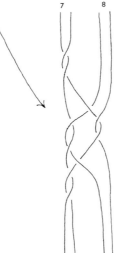

2.27 Fishtails, detail of 2.26

After pin C (see 2.28):
Work two 'eyes' into the row, using
passive prs 5, 6, 7 & 8 from each side
(see 2.26), thus:
< Tw 2 prs 6 & 7,

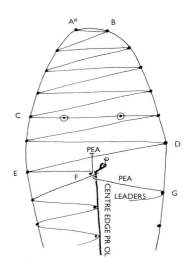

2.28 Fishtails, splitting braid; adding centre pr and new leaders

X T T X with prs 5 & 6, leave
(see 2.27)
X T T X with prs 7 & 8, leave
Tw 2 prs 6 & 7 >
Rep < to > at the other side of the
braid
Note: This method of making holes
will keep the colours in order. Some
careful help in opening out the holes,
with a pin or back of a crochet hook,
may be required.

After pin D:
Prepare to split braid. Since the total
number of prs is odd, add 1 pr PEA to
become central passive pr (26 prs)
Note: Split braid, variation. A
variation may be used (though not in
this design) to split a braid if the total
number of prs is even; take the
existing central passive pr as the new
leaders, work to the next pin and
change the colour of the leaders if
required.

After pin E (see 2.28):
Edge st, work leaders thro 1 pr, use a
locking st (X T X T X) to hold work
secure.

Leave

Just above pinhole F, on a temp pin, hang 1 pr OL to be centre edge pr (27 prs)

SPLIT BRAID thus:

Cls central passive pr PEA, to become new leaders, thro centre edge pr OL (on temp pin) placing pin F after X T of X T X Cls

Tw 2 both prs

Remove temp pin

Note: Now the leader pr for the right side of fish is the former central passive pr PEA.

Cont working right side of fish:

T O & T B 1 pr *SIL/FL, 2nd passive from centre edge (26 prs)

Work 1st row patt Dewdrops, dividing passives into 3 sets of 3 prs

Cls & Tw 1st passive pr next to right edge pr (see 2.29)

Place pin G

Make locking st with 1st passive pr (X T X T X)

Leave

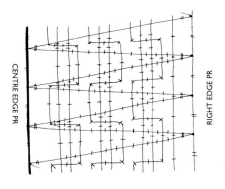

2.29 Fishtails, Dewdrops pattern

RETURN to pin E:

Note: Remember, the left side of the fish must be worked first, as the centre edge will be rolled back. The right side of the fish will be joined to the

rolled centre edge with top sewings.

Undo the locking st at pin E

Adjust the tension on the prs

T O & T B 2 passive prs, no 4 *SIL/FL & no 7 **W/FL from left edge

Start patt Ribbon

Divide passives into 4 sets of 2 prs

Cls & Tw 1st passive pr next to centre edge pr (see 2.30)

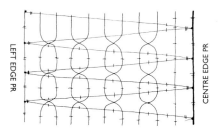

2.30 Fishtails, Ribbon pattern

After pin H:

Before Cls sets tog as in patt, change passive pr no 2 (*MAU/*PIG) to *PAN, thus:

< Hang new pr (*PAN) on temp pin

Cls old pr (*MAU/*PIG) thro new pr

T O & T B old pr.

Cont with new pr in patt (see 2.31) >

Change passive pr no 4 (*SIL) to *MAU

Rep < to >

Change passive pr no 6 (FL) to *SIL

Rep < to >

Change passive pr no 8 (**W) to FL

Rep < to >

After pin I:

Before Cls sets tog as in patt (see 2.31)

Change passive pr no 4 (*SIL/FL) to *PAN

Rep < to >

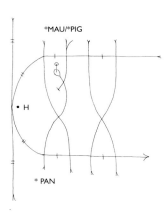

2.31 Fishtails, changing pattern prs in pattern

Change passive pr no 6 (**W/FL) to *MAU

Rep < to >

Change passive pr no 8 (FL/**W) to *SIL

Rep < to >

After pin J:

As patt, Cls sets tog

T O & T B passive pr no 7 (FL)

Cont in patt, Cls & Tw rem pr from 4th set (before Cls & Tw last passive pr before centre edge)

After pin K:

T O & T B passive pr no 7 (*SIL)

Also, as before, change passive pr no 2 (*MAU/*PIG) to *DEL

After pin L:

Change passive pr no 3 (*MAU) to *DEL

After pin M:

Change passive pr no 6 (*SIL) to *DEL

After pin N:

Change passive pr no 2 (*MAU) to *HEL

After pin O:
Change passive pr no 1 (*DEL) to
PUR and passive pr no 4 (*DEL) to
*HEL

After pin P:
Change passive pr no 3 (*MAU) to
PUR and passive pr no 6 (*DEL) to
*HEL

After pin Q:
Change passive pr no 5 (*MAU) to
PUR

After pin R:
Change leaders FL to *HEL
(see 1.18)
Patt across to pin S
Tw 2 leaders,
Pin S (see 2.32)
Again, change leaders *HEL with
right edge pr OL
X T X & Tw 2 new right edge pr
*HEL (see 1.47)
Hang 1 pr *SKY on a temp pin
(see 2.32)
Cls pr OL thro *SKY
Tw 2 *SKY and remove temp pin
T O & T B pr OL
Note: This pr OL will be used for roll
later.

Untwist 1st passive pr FL/**W
Hang 1 pr OL on a temp pin
Cls pr FL/**W thro pr OL
T O & T B pr FL/**W
Cls new leaders *SKY thro new 1st
passive pr OL (10 prs)
Cont in patt Ribbon with PUR/*HEL
prs, changing to Cls & Tw when
PUR/*HEL area becomes very narrow
Cont in Cls with the newly added
GREEN prs thus:
Between pins S and T, add 3 prs in
order as foll:
1 pr APP
1 pr PEA
1 pr *MIN
at the same time
T O & T B prs from the left edge

until 7 prs worked in Cls rem, in order
as foll:
Left edge pr 2 x *HEL
2 x OL
2 x APP
2 x PEA
2 x *MIN
Right edge pr 2 x *HEL
Leaders 2 x *SKY (7 prs)

After pin T:
Cls thro 1st passive pr and use a
locking st to secure threads in position
while the roll and the right side of the
fish are worked
Return to pin S (and the T O & T B
1 pr OL)

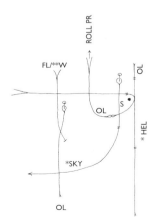

2.32 Fishtails, saving the edge pr for use in roll,
changing leaders and changing passive prs in pattern

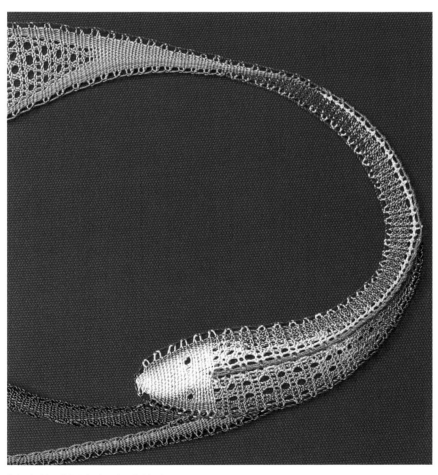

Fishtails (detail). Fish body with rolled back spine

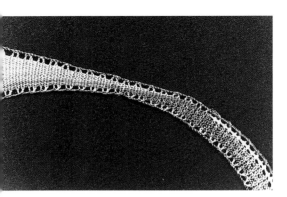

Fishtails (detail). Braid and colour changes, also commencement of roll back along spine of fish

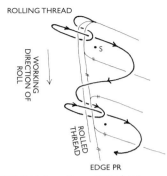

2.33 Fishtails, working a (Withof) roll

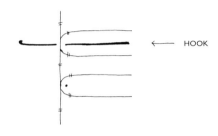

2.34 Fishtails, direction of insertion of crochet hook

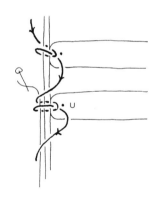

2.35 Fishtails, adding a thread to a (Withof) roll

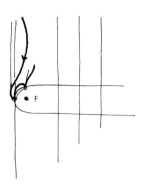

2.36 Fishtails, finishing a (Withof) roll

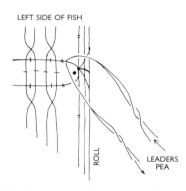

2.37 Fishtails, top sewings to join braid over roll

To roll (see also rolling notes, Crocus Leaves, section 1, after pin I, and diagrams 2.10, 2.11 and 2.12):
In this example, remove pin S, insert very fine 0.4mm crochet hook into work under the edge prs, as if making a side sewing, and one of the threads from the pr OL. The other thread from the pr OL will be the rolling thread
Rep from < to > after pin I, section 1, Crocus Leaves, until pin F is reached (see 2.33 & 2.35)

However, at pin U:
Add 1 single thread APP on temp pin to be included in the roll (see 2.35) alongside the existing roll thread
Note: In this example, keep the lighter threads to the outer edge of the roll.

At pin V:
In the same way, add another 1 single thread APP to be included in the roll (see 2.35)
Note: When adding single threads to a roll, leave them attached to temp pins until the roll has been finished off. Keep roll even by pulling the roll threads gently but firmly, after each pinhole has been worked, and pushing the pins right down into the pillow.

After pin W:
T B 1 single thread OL

After pin X:
T B 1 single thread APP
Note: When T B single threads it is not usually necessary to tie them off, unless the piece is likely to be disturbed by continuing work.

At pin F, to finish roll (see 2.36):
Make side sewing to attach roll, then make top sewing into the bar of the same pinhole
T O & T B both threads

RETURN to pin G:
Undo the locking st, and adjust tension
Cont in patt Dewdrops
Join right side of fish to centre edge, over roll, with top sewings (see 2.37)

After pin Y:
Where braid narrows, after a 4 row patt sequence has been completed and prs have returned to their original start position, T O & T B 2nd passive pr from right edge

Work back to centre edge in Cls &
Tw and sew into lower bar from
previous pinhole (blind pin)
Patt passives 1–6 from centre edge
Cls & Tw rem prs to right edge
Cont in this way, decreasing prs from
near right edge, leaving 1st passive pr
from right edge intact to maintain an
even line to body of fish.
When part of a Dewdrops 3 pr set
must be decreased, Cls & Tw rem prs
keeping the original colour order
found at the beginning of patt

At pin Z:
Change leaders PEA to *S.F. thus:
Work to pin Z
Make top sewing into top bar with old
leaders
T O & T B old leaders
Add new leaders to lower bar, Tw 2
and cont to right edge
Pin and edge st
Return to centre edge, changing
passive prs (order seen L to R):
 FL to *PIG
*SKY to *DEL
*MIN to *S.F.
Thus:
Hang new pr on temp pin
Cls old pr thro new pr
T O & T B old pr
Carefully remove temp pin
Lower new pr into position and cont.
Work to right edge, decreasing
Pin and edge st
Return to centre edge, changing
passive prs (order seen L to R):
FL/*SIL to *MAU
*MIN to OL
as before
Work to right edge, decreasing
Pin and edge st
Return to centre edge, changing
passive pr:

*PIG to *HEL
as before
Work to right edge, decreasing
Pin and edge st
Return to centre edge, changing
passive pr
*MAU to PUR
as before

At pin A1:
Change leaders * S.F. to * OL1, see
pin Z (see 2.38) L to R order should
be as foll:
Leaders 2 x *OLI
2 x *HEL
2 x PUR
2 x OL
*DEL
*PIG
Right edge pr 2 x *OLI (6 prs)
Note: This order need not be exact.
Cont to pin U in Cls & Tw,
decreasing
To finish, T O & T B rem prs and
secure to work

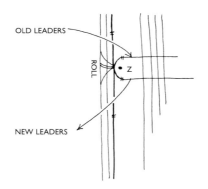

2.38 Fishtails, changing leaders, over roll,
by top sewings

RETURN to pin T (see 2.39):
Undo locking st, Cls 3 prs
Cls left edge pr *HEL with 1st passive
pr APP
Tw 2 pr APP
Cls leaders *SKY thro pr *HEL, Tw 2

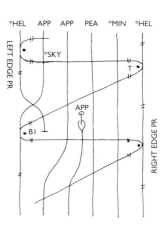

2.39 Fishtails, changing edge pr with passive pr, and
adding passive pr

leaders
At pin B1 (see 2.39):
Edge st with pr APP
T O & T B old left edge pr *HEL
Add 1 pr APP on temp pin, to
become 2nd passive from left edge
(7 prs)
Cont in Cls to pin C1, adding prs as
foll:
1 pr PEA
1 pr PEA
1 pr *MIN
1 pr PEA
1 pr *MIN
to give order L to R as foll:
Left edge pr 2 x OL
2 x APP
2 x PEA
2 x APP
4 x PEA
2 x *MIN
2 x PEA
4 x *MIN
Right edge pr 2 x *HEL
Leaders 2 x *SKY (12 prs)

After pin C1:
Cont in Cls to pin D1, adding prs as
foll:
1 pr *SKY
1 pr *SKY

1 pr *SKY
1 pr *MIN
1 pr *SKY
1 pr *HY
1 pr *PAN
to give order L to R as foll:
Left edge pr 2 x OL
2 x APP
2 x PEA
2 x APP
4 PEA
2 x *MIN
2 x PEA
2 x *MIN
2 x *SKY
2 x *MIN
2 x *SKY
2 x *MIN
2 x *SKY
2 x *HY
2 x *SKY
2 x *PAN
Right edge pr 2 x *HEL
Leaders 2 x *SKY (19 prs)

After pin D1:
Cont to add 1 pr to right edge at next
2 pins;
1 pr *MAU to be 1st passive, then
1 pr *PAN to be 1st passive (21 prs)
At the same time start patt Lattice 3,
variation (see Crocus, section 2,
diagram 2.20)
Cls tog passive prs 9 *SKY and 10
*MIN from the left side (see 2.40)
Cls thro 8 passive prs, Tw 1 leaders
Cls leaders thro 1 pr, Tw 1 leaders
Rep * to * once more
Cls to right edge and cont in patt as
in patt diagram 2.40 to pin E1

After pin E1 (see 2.41):
Change to Cls & Tw

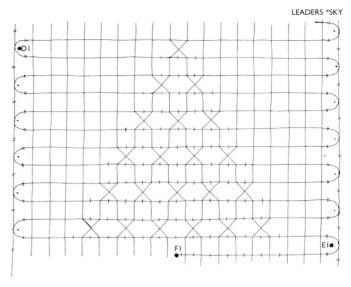

2.40 *Fishtails, shaped section of Lattice 3, variation at pin D1*

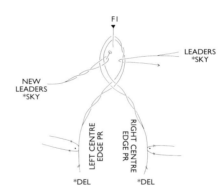

2.41 *Fishtails, adding new leaders and centre edge prs*

Work to centre pin F1, from right
edge
Hang 2 prs *DEL on pin F1, Tw 2

WORK LEFT SIDE OF TAIL thus:
On temp pin, hang new leaders pr
*SKY
Cls leaders thro pr hanging from left
side of pin F1.
Work to left edge in Cls & Tw with
new leaders *SKY
Leave

WORK RIGHT SIDE OF TAIL thus:
Take old leaders *SKY from right side
of fish, worked from pin E1, Tw 2
Take this pr leaders over and under
right pr *DEL hanging from pin F1,
and work back to right edge
Cls & Tw tog both prs *DEL hanging
at pin F1
Note: A ½ knot may be tied with each
of these prs to keep the threads close
to the pin.
The centre edge prs are *DEL
Each side of the fish is now worked
independently.
Gradually return to Cls as braid
narrows, omitting twist from near the
outer sides first.

RETURN TO LEFT SIDE OF TAIL:
Cont in Cls gradually reducing prs, by
T O & T B passive prs from near
centre edge, keeping 1st passive pr
from left edge intact, but changing
leaders *SKY with passive pr PEA,
when pr PEA is 2nd passive pr from

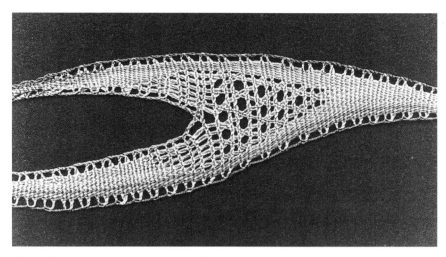

Fishtails (detail). Lattice 3, variation and splitting of braid

the centre edge (see 2.42)

T O & T B old leaders *SKY

Cont with new leaders PEA (7 prs)

Order L to R as foll:

Left edge pr 2 x OL

2 x APP

2 x PEA

2 x APP

PEA

*MIN

Right edge pr 2 x *DEL

Leaders 2 x PEA (7 prs)

After pin G1:

Add prs from left edge and reduce prs from centre edge, to give order L to R as foll:

Left edge pr 2 x OL

2 x *OLI

2 x OL

2 x APP

Centre edge pr 2 x *DEL

Leaders 2 x PEA (6 prs)

After pin H1:

Change leaders PEA to APP

(see 1.18)

At pin I1 (see 2.43):

Change left edge pr OL to *OLI (also see 2.39)

Before making up edge st at pin I1,

add 1 pr *OLI on temp pin

Cls old edge pr OL thro new pr *OLI

T O & T B pr OL

Cls leaders to edge

Pin I1 and edge st, cont

Order L to R as foll:

Left edge pr 2 x *OLI

2 x *OLI

2 x OL

2 x APP

Centre edge pr 2 x *DEL

Leaders 2 x APP (6 prs)

At pin J1:

Edge st and use locking st with 1st passive pr

RETURN TO RIGHT SIDE OF TAIL:

Cont in Cls, gradually reducing prs, by T O & T B passive prs from near centre edge, also adding prs to right edge to give following order shown, but exchanging leaders *SKY with passive pr *PAN, when *PAN is 2nd passive pr from centre edge (see 2.42)

Order L to R as foll:

Centre edge pr 2 x *DEL

2 x *SKY

2 x *MAU

2 x *PAN

2 x PUR

Right edge pr 2 x *HEL

Leaders 2 x *HEL (7 prs)

At pin K1:

Change leaders *PAN to *HEL

(see 1.18)

Change to Tenstick (see 1.49)

T O & T B 1 pr *SKY (6 prs)

T O & T B 1 pr *PAN (5 prs)

After pin L1 (see 2.44):

Join the two braids tog in Tenstick thus:

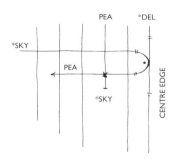

2.42 Fishtails, changing leaders with passive prs

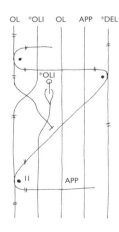

2.43 Fishtails, changing edge pr with passive pr and adding new passive pr

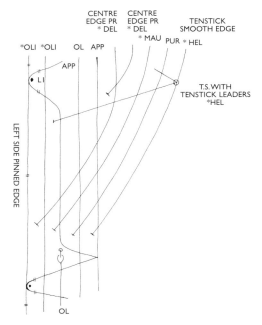

CENTRE EDGE PR * DEL   CENTRE EDGE PR * DEL   TENSTICK SMOOTH EDGE

*OLI *OLI   OL   APP   * MAU   PUR * HEL

APP

• LI

LEFT SIDE PINNED EDGE

T.S. WITH TENSTICK LEADERS *HEL

OL

2.44 Fishtails, joining two braids together in Tenstick

Work to smooth edge, and make T.S.
Leave
Cls both *DEL central edge prs tog
T O & T B *DEL edge pr from right
side of tail
Cls left side of tail leaders APP thro
1st passive pr *OLI
Take leader pr from Tenstick smooth
edge and Cls thro 5 prs to the left
Cls this Tenstick leader with leader
APP from left side braid
T O & T B Tenstick leader
Cls 4 prs from left side thro 4 prs from
right side Tenstick
T O & T B all 4 prs from Tenstick
Take leaders APP (now 2nd pr on
left) thro 1 more pr to the right
Work T.S. at the smooth edge on
right and cont in Tenstick
Add 1 pr OL to be 2nd passive from
pinned edge (6 prs)

After pin N1:
Add 1 pr *OLI to be 2nd passive pr
from pinned edge (7 prs)

After pin O1:
Change leaders APP and smooth edge
pr APP to *OLI
Follow instructions and diagrams 2.6,
2.7 & 2.8 repeating diagram 2.6
When pin P1 is reached, change from
Tenstick smooth edge to a pinned
edge (see 1.50)
Add 2 prs *OLI
T O & T B 1 pr OL to give order L to
R as foll:
Left edge pr 2 x *OLI
4 x *OLI
2 x OL
4 x *OLI
Right edge pr 2 x *OLI
Leaders 2 x *OLI (8 prs)

After pin Q:
Change to ½ st, retaining 1 pr
passives, at each side of braid, to be
worked in Cls as a 1st passive pr

After pin R1:
Add 1 pr *HEL, from right side
(see 2.45)
Cls *HEL thro 1st passive pr *OLI,
Tw 1 *HEL
Cont in ½ st

After pin S1:
Add 1 pr PUR, from right side as
before (see 2.45) (10 prs)

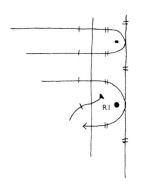

R1

2.45 Fishtails, adding passive pr at edge in ½ st

After pin T1:
Add 1 pr *OLI, from right side as
before (see 2.45)

After pin U1:
Add 1 pr *HEL, from right side as
before (see 2.45)

After pin V1:
Add 1 pr *CLI, from right side as
before (see 2.45)

After pin W1:
Add 1 pr PUR, from right side as
before (see 2.45) (14 prs)

SPLIT BRAID thus (see 2.46):
After pin X1:
Work edge st and locking st with 1st
passive pr. Leave
Make ½ st with passives 5 & 6
On temp pin, hang 2 prs *OLI Tw 5

WORK RIGHT SIDE:
Undo locking st
Take leaders in ½ st towards centre
fish shape
Work T.S. with right pr *OLI from
temp pin, using a support pin Y1
(after X T of X T X T X)
Work back to right side edge, pin Z1,
edge st and make locking st. Leave

RETURN TO LEFT SIDE at pin A2
(see 2.47):
Add 1 pr new leaders *OLI, using a
top sewing into the lower bar at
pin A2
Cls new leaders *OLI thro 1st
passive pr
Tw 1 new leaders
Take new leaders in ½ st to centre fish
shape (see 2.46)
Work T.S. with left pr *OLI from
temp pin, using support pin B2 (after

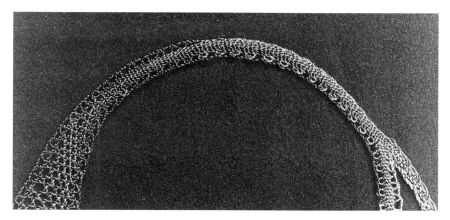

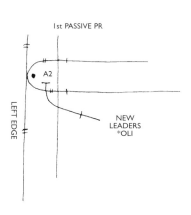

Fishtails (detail). Joining Tenstick braid and pinned edge together, continuing in Tenstick then changing to a pinned edge braid

2.47 Fishtails, adding new leaders to previously worked pin using top sewing

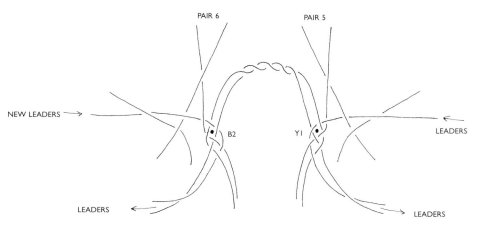

2.46 Fishtails, splitting ½ st braid, adding centre edge prs for supported Tenstick edge

After pin F2:

Add 1 pr APP to be 1st passive pr from the smooth edge

T O & T B 1 pr containing *HEL/PUR or *OLI, leaving 1 pr *OLI as 1st passive pr next to the pinned edge

After pin G2:

Add 1 pr PEA to be single passives 1 & 3 from smooth edge

T O & T B 1 pr *HEL/PUR or *OLI

Order should be L to R as foll:

Smooth edge pr 2 x OL

PEA

APP

PEA

APP

X T of X T X T X)

Work back to left side edge, pin C2, edge st and make locking st. Leave

RETURN TO RIGHT SIDE:

Undo locking st and cont in ½ st, working a supported T.S. smooth edge at the centre edge

After pin D2:

Change to Cls. Work 2 rows

Cont to work a supported T.S. smooth edge at the centre edge

Where necessary, change leaders and smooth edge pr to OL

Follow instructions and diagrams 2.6, 2.7 & 2.8, repeating diagram 2.6

After pin E2:

Add 2 prs OL to be 1st passive prs from the smooth edge at each addition

T O & T B 2 prs containing *HEL and/or PUR from near the smooth edge

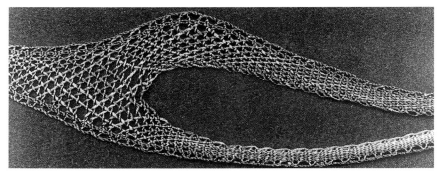

Fishtails (detail). Splitting braid in ½ st, and working a supported Tenstick edge

4 x OL

2 x *OLI

Pinned (right) edge pr 2 x *OLI

Leaders 2 x OL (8 prs)

After pin H2:

Add 1 pr APP to be single passives

5 & 7 from pinned edge (9 prs)

Change from Tenstick to Cls with a

pinned edge (see 1.50)

Join to head of fish with top sewings

RETURN TO LEFT SIDE at pin C2:

Cont in ½ st, still maintaining the

supported T.S. smooth edge for the

central fish shape

To finish:

Use top sewings to join to head of fish

and right side of central fish shape, at

pin H2

T O & T B rem prs in a bunch

KNOT ONE, BUT TWO

The knot motif is featured in several of the following patterns. On each of the occasions the pricking is identical, but the working instructions differ.

This version is worked very simply. Neither the leaders nor the passive threads change colour whilst working; they are allowed to work through the pattern from their original starting positions. This illustrates how subtle shading effects can be achieved when using a good tonal range of threads. One half of each knot is one tone darker than the other, and there is a progression of tones so that on completion of both motifs four tonal relationships can be seen. The green threads used in sections 2 and 4 are identical. The leaders, however, are different and relate to their relevant halves.

COLOUR TONAL VALUE CHART

Knot One

Section	1	2	3	4
Light tone (LT)	EC	EC	*IV	*IV
L. Med tone (LMT)	*IV		*BLU	
D. Med tone (DMT)	*BLU	OL	*ROS	OL
Dark tone (DT)	*ROS	*OLI	*STR	*OLI

But Two

Section	1	2	3	4
Light tone (LT)	*BLU	*BLU	*ROS	*ROS
L. Med tone (LMT)	*ROS		*STR	
D. Med tone (DMT)	*STR	OL	*HIB	OL
Dark tone (DT)	*HIB	*OLI	CRA	*OLI

Although the actual colours used in Knot One are given in the written instructions, they are shown in the diagrams as tonal values (see the colour tonal value chart above). Note: The tonal values of the threads in each section change, depending upon which colours are in use. For example, in section 1, the Light tone is ECru and the L. Med tone is *IVory. However, since section 3 is to be one tone darker overall, ECru is not used here and therefore *IVory becomes the Light tone. When working, check each section with the aforementioned colour tonal value chart.

Pricking Size: See 2.48

100%: Pipers Silks

80/3 Spun silk

*90/3 Gloss silk

Thread: Pipers Silks (see Pricking notes) 80/3 and *90/3 are shown in the samples. See Thread notes for Crocus Leaves and Crocus.

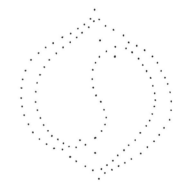

2.48 Knot One, But Two, pricking

Colours: Ecru EC

*Ivory *IV

*Blush *BLU

*Rose *ROS

*Strawberry *STR

*Hibiscus *HIB

Cranberry CRA

Olive OL

*Olive *OLI

Note: * denotes 90/3 Gloss silk; all other threads are 80/3 Spun silk.

Techniques: No (colour) change edge stitch

One-colour point start

Magic threads

Blending colours/threads

Turning stitch

Blind pins

Point finish, decreasing from a wide
angle, after T.S.

Roll (Withof)

Adding & decreasing coloured
threads, roll (Withof)

Narrow-angle start

Top sewings

Stitches and Braids: Cloth stitch
Ovals
Ribbon

To Work: Work each section
numerically as shown in 2.49. No
(colour) change edge st is used
throughout. Top sewings are used
throughout. Colours/threads are
shown singly in thread order listings,
unless otherwise indicated. Actual
colours given in written instructions;
tonal values given in diagrams. Refer
to colour tonal value chart.

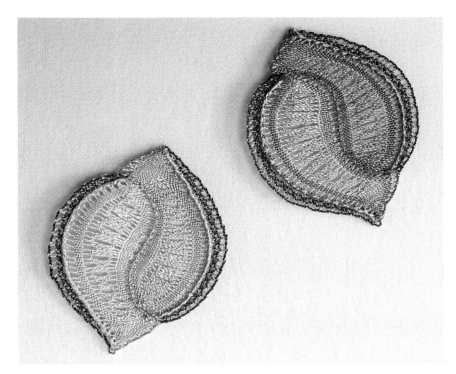

Knot One, But Two. Pipers Silks 80/3 and 90/3

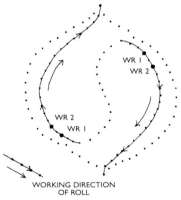

2.50 Knot One, But Two, working direction of roll

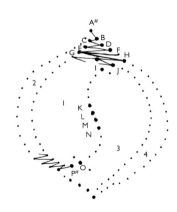

*2.49 Knot One, But Two, pin reference plan and
working order*

SECTION 1 (SEE 2.48 & 2.49)

START at pin A# (one-colour point
start):

Hang 2 prs *ROS open on pin A #,

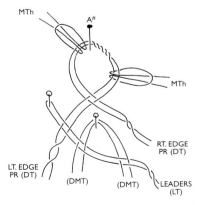

*2.51 Knot One, But Two, one-colour point start, with
magic threads*

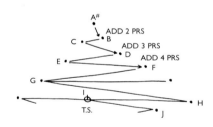

*2.52 Knot One, But Two, start detail, adding prs,
magic threads and start of pattern*

Tw 5 (see 2.51)

Place 2 magic threads around prs,
before Cls

Cls leaders EC L to R thro left edge pr

Tw 2 left edge pr

Cls leaders thro 2 prs *BLU, Tw 2
leaders

Pin B & edge st. Cont in Cls
(see 2.52)

At pin C:

Place a magic thread either side of the
pin

Pin C to pin D:

Add 3 prs

Pin E to pin F:

Add 4 prs

Blend colours to give order as foll:

Edge pr 2 x *ROS

2 x *BLU

*IV

*BLU

*IV

EC

*IV

EC

Centre pr 2 x EC

Leaders 2 x EC

Repeat threads from centre pr to edge pr (12 prs)

At pin G:

Work a blind pin

After pin H:

Place a magic thread around leaders at edge

Tie ½ knot with leaders after 1st passive pr (see 2.52)

Work to centre pin I

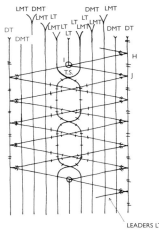

2.53 Knot One, But Two, Ovals pattern and tonal colour positions

Make T.S. with centre passive pr EC (see 2.53)

Begin patt Ovals

Place magic thread at pin J

Work blind pins at pins K, L, M & N

After 8 patt repeats, work to centre, make T.S. using support pin.

Change to Cls, decreasing from centre

Note: Do not cut off prs yet, they will

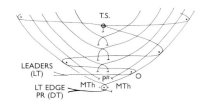

2.54 Knot One, But Two, point finish decreasing prs from wide angle after T.S.

be used to tie back prs later (see 2.54).

After pin O:

Cls thro 2 prs.

T O & T B leaders to use for roll

At pin P#:

Cls with edge prs, pin P# and place a magic thread around each edge pr

Cls edge prs to close pin P#

T O & T B right pr and secure to

work with previously T O & T B prs

Tie ½ knot in left pr and use in roll

Place leaders EC between left pr

*ROS, tie a knot.

Note: In this design the lightest tone is used as the rolling thread to attach the roll.

Included in the roll: 1 thread to match the rolling thread, 2 threads Dark tone and, additionally, 1 thread Dark Med tone, 1 thread Light Med tone.

To roll (see 2.10 & 2.11):

Use rolling thread EC to enclose roll threads; 1 thread EC, 2 threads *ROS (see 2.50)

At pin WR 1:

Add 1 thread *BLU

At pin WR 2:

Add 1 thread *IV

To finish roll:

In this design, decrease 1 thread at each pin in order:

Dark tone

Dark Med tone

Dark tone

Light Med tone,

to leave 1 rolling thread (EC) and 1 roll thread (EC)

Roll into the last pinhole, pin A#, using one of the magic threads (see Crocus, section 2, diagram 2.19)

T O both prs

Take 1 pr back to previous pinhole (pin C, section 1)

Use one of the magic threads and make a top sewing

T O & T B both rem prs again (this will keep the remaining threads away from the point so they will be invisible when the work is viewed

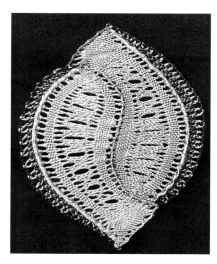

Knot One, But Two. Rolled edges.
Braids: Ovals and Ribbon

from the correct side)

Note: The remaining magic thread from pin A# will be used at the start of section 2.

SECTION 2 (SEE 2.49)

Start at pin P# (narrow-angle start, see 2.13)

Note: Blind pins are not worked in this section; the design allows for the leaders to work at an angle which emphasizes the curved shape of the knot.

Use magic thread to start, hang on right edge pr *OLI, leaders EC and 1 passive pr *OLI (3 prs)

Work to edge, pin & edge st

Work back towards rolled edge, adding 1 passive pr OL to centre of braid (4 prs)

Make top sewings into rolled edge

Begin patt ribbon, using one set of two prs (see 2.56)

When the braid narrows, 5th pin from finish, T O & T B 1 pr OL

Cls remaining pr *OLI.

After using the remaining magic thread at the pin before the point to make a top sewing (pin C, section 1) T O & T B leaders and passive pr

At the point pin A#, using the magic thread, sew in right edge pr

T O & T B and secure to work using previously discarded prs

SECTION 3 (SEE 2.49)

Note: Section 3 is identical to section 1.

Work as section 1, top sewing into previously worked sections, using thread order as foll:

Edge pr 2 x *STR

2 x *ROS

*BLU

*ROS

*BLU

*IV

*BLU

*IV

Centre pr 2 x *IV

Leaders 2 x *IV

Repeat threads from centre pr to edge pr (12 prs)

At pin H:

T O right edge pr after joining section 2, ensuring that it is enclosed between the leaders

Tie ½ knot, and T B edge pr

Also at pin H:

After the 1st passive pr, tie ½ knot

Pin J:

Repeat * to *

When the left edge pr uses the magic thread to sew into the last pinhole, replace the magic thread (it will be needed to start section 4)

SECTION 4 (SEE 2.49)

Note: Section 4 is identical to section 2.

Work as section 2, top sewing into previously worked sections, using thread order as foll:

Right edge pr *OLI

1 passive pr *OLI

Leaders *IV

1 pr added OL (4 prs)

STRING OF PEARLS

Exactly the same pricking is used for the pearls in this design as is used for the knot in Knot One, But Two. However, as different braids are featured, the working instructions are also different.

The sample shows the design worked with only five pearls, but there

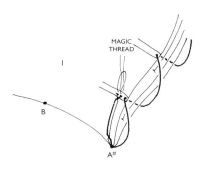

2.55 *Knot One, But Two, decreasing from a roll and finishing at a point*

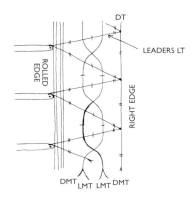

2.56 *Knot One, But Two, section 2 narrow braid, Ribbon pattern*

is an additional section which allows for a further two pearls to extend the necklace (see 2.58).

Although fourteen different coloured threads have been used for this piece, it is possible to work the piece using only six. Each pearl, although subtly different in the example, actually only needs six different coloured threads.

Each half of the pearl needs three tonal shades: light, medium and dark. Essentially the light shade is used as a highlight, so sometimes the colour used may not actually be noticeably lighter, simply more intense, e.g. in sections 3 and 4 where Purple is used as the highlight although it is tonally similar to *Helio. Equally, the dark tones used may borrow the dark tone from the other half pearl, e.g. section 2, part of the green half, has borrowed Navy, the dark tone from the blue half, to use alongside Dark Tartan; section 4, part of the blue half, has borrowed Dark Tartan, the dark tone from the green half, to use alongside Navy. This gives a richer and more cohesive feel to the work because the colours are related to the whole.

Where the pearls are much lighter in tone, the highlights have been kept to the lightest tone, i.e. **White. The more intense and saturated colours have generally been reserved for the darker tones, e.g. in section 5, where *Ivory and Pale Lime are of a similar tone, Pale Lime is used as the darkest tone, with the addition of *Mint, borrowed from sections 7 and 8, used in section 6. This is shown in the colour tonal value chart.

To emphasize the difference further between the dark and the light pearls, the black pearl, sections 1–4, has Lattice 1 as its main braid pattern whereas the other pearls have Lattice 3, variation.

In the sample here, the connecting string is worked along one side in Tenstick, then some of the pairs are rolled back along the pinned edge, and another section of Tenstick is worked to match the first. You can instead work a very narrow section of a Milanese braid, but that requires additional and substituted pinholes. (See also introductory notes from Knot One, But Two.)

Pricking Size: See 2.57 & 2.58
100%: Pipers Silks
80/3 Spun silks
*90/3 Gloss silks
**300 Semi-gloss (white)

COLOUR TONAL VALUE CHART

Section	Light Tone	Med Tone	Dark Tone
1	*H.B.	G.BL	D.TAR
2	*H.B.	G.BL	D.TAR (& NAV)
3	PUR	*HEL	NAV
4	PUR	*HEL	NAV (& D.TAR)
5	**W	*IV	P.LI
6	**W	*IV	P.LI (& *MIN)
7	**W	*WAT	*MIN
8	**W	*WAT	*MIN (& P.LI)
9	**W	FL	*WAT
10	**W	FL	*WAT (& *SIL)
11	**W	P.LI	*SIL
12	**W	P.LI	*SIL (& *WAT)
13	**W	FL	*SIL
14	**W	FL	*SIL (& *IV)
15	**W	FL	*IV
16	**W	FL	*IV (& *SIL)
17	**W	EC	*SIL
18	**W	EC	*SIL (& *IV)
19	**W	EC	*IV
20	**W	EC	*IV (& *SIL)

( ) denotes borrowed colours; see introductory notes and diagrams 2.66 & 2.68.

Thread: Pipers (see Pricking notes), 80/3, *90/3 and **300 Semi-gloss (white) are shown in the sample. See Thread notes for Crocus Leaves and Crocus.

Colours: *Honeybird H.B.
Green-Blue G.BL
Dark Tartan D.TAR
Navy NAV
Purple PUR
*Helio *HEL
**White **W
*Ivory *IV
Pale Lime P.LI
*Mint *MIN
*Water *WAT
Flesh FL

*Silver *SIL
Ecru EC
Note: * denotes 90/3 Gloss silk, ** denotes 300 Semi-gloss (white); all other threads are 80/3 Spun silk.

Techniques: No (colour) change edge
  stitch
Two-colour point start (variation)
Magic threads
Blending colours/threads
Blind pins
Changing passive patt threads
Point finish, decreasing from a wide
  angle
Roll (Withof)
Adding & decreasing coloured
  threads, roll (Withof)

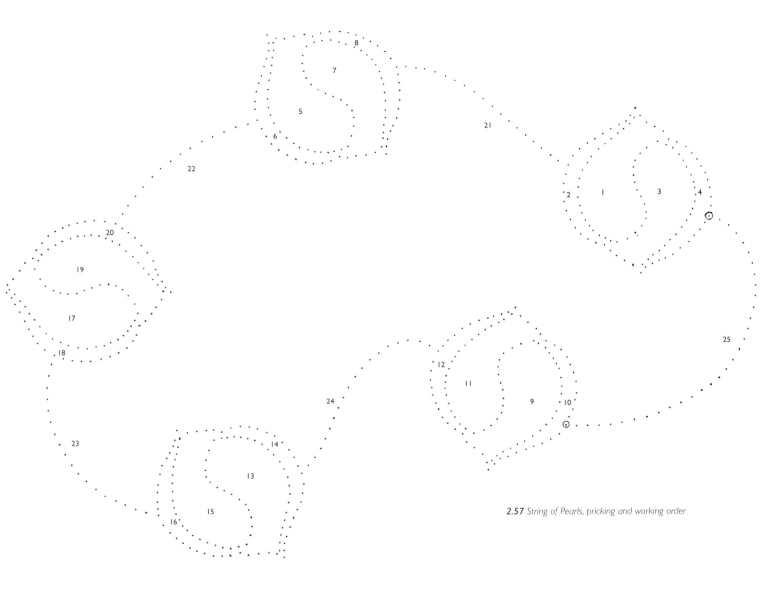

2.57 String of Pearls, pricking and working order

Narrow-angle start
Top sewings
Transferring threads from roll to
   another section

Stitches and Braids: Cloth stitch
Cloth stitch & twist
Lattice 1
Ribbon
Lattice 3 (variation)
Tenstick

To Work: Work each section
numerically as shown in 2.57 and

2.58. No (colour) change edge st is
used throughout. Top sewings are used
throughout. Colours/threads are
shown singly in thread order listings,
unless otherwise indicated. Refer to
colour tonal value chart.
Option: If the extended version is to
be worked, section 25, the string, from
the smaller version is omitted and
replaced by section 25, part of a pearl,
from the extended version, which is
now the next section to be worked.
Note: The colours have not been
given for the extended section.

Use magic threads in the same way
and at the same places as given for
Knot One, But Two.

SECTION 1 (SEE 2.57 & 2.59)

START at pin A# (two-colour point
start – variation):
Note: Refer to colour tonal value
chart and diagram 2.63 for colours.
Hang 2 prs side by side on pin A#
(see 2.61)
Tw 2 right edge pr
Cls leaders thro left edge pr

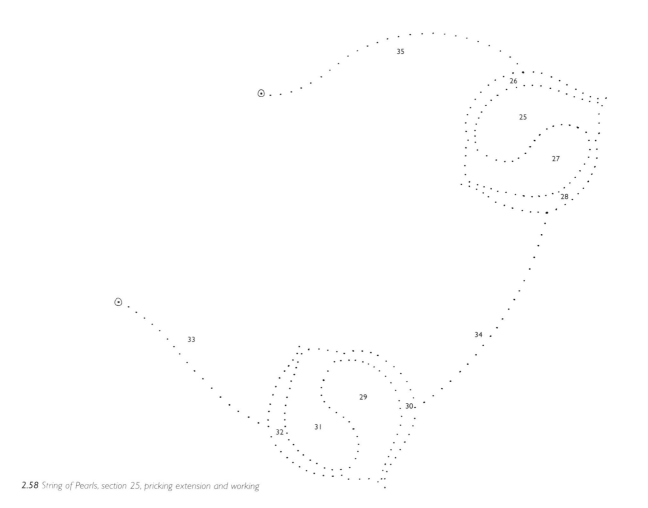

2.58 String of Pearls, section 25, pricking extension and working

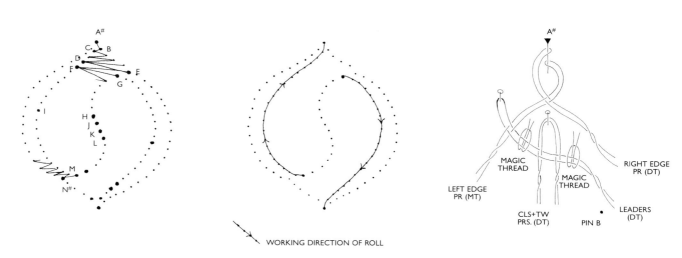

WORKING DIRECTION OF ROLL

2.59 String of Pearls, pin reference plan

2.60 String of Pearls, working direction of roll

2.61 String of Pearls, two-colour point start (variation), magic threads and showing colour tones for sections 1 & 3

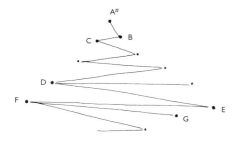

2.62 *String of Pearls, start detail*

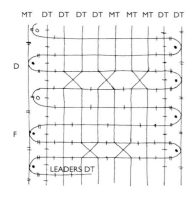

2.63 *String of Pearls, detail, start of pattern, Lattice 1 for sections 1 & 3, and all following odd-numbered sections*

Tw 2 left edge pr
Place magic thread around leaders
Cls & Tw leaders thro 2 prs on temp pin
Place another magic thread around leaders
Tw 2 leaders
Place pin B, & edge st (see 2.62)
Place a magic thread either side of pin C
Cont adding 6 more prs worked in Cls, in between the 2 Cls & Tw prs, before pin D, to give order shown (see 2.63) (11 prs)

After pin D, the 1st blind pin has been completely worked:
Start patt Lattice 1 (see 1.12), working Cls & Tw with 1 pr at either side of braid, and using 3 sets of 2 prs for patt (see 2.63)

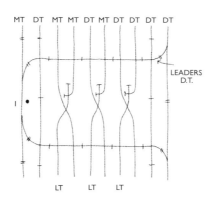

2.64 *String of Pearls, changing prs in pattern Lattice 1, sections 1 & 3*

Place a magic thread after edge st at pin E
Work another blind pin at pin F
Place a magic thread at pin G
Work a blind pin at pin H

After pin I (see 2.64):
Before Cls prs tog in patt; to add highlights, change the right pr of each set to the lightest tone thus:
Hang new prs on temp pins
Cls new prs thro old prs
T O & T B old prs
Remove temp pins and cont in patt
Cls prs tog (see 2.64)
Work a blind pin at each of pins J, K & L
Towards the end of the braid, change the passive threads back to their original order and cont in Cls
Decrease passive prs where braid narrows (see 2.65)

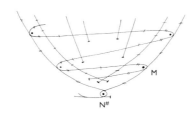

2.65 *String of Pearls, wide-angle point finish*

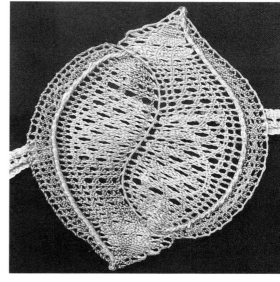

String of Pearls (detail). Lattice 3, variation

After pin M:
Work leaders thro 2 Cls & Tw prs
T O & T B leaders
Cls tog 2 Cls & Tw prs
T O & T B both prs

At pin N#:
Cls edge prs tog, pin N#
place a magic thread around each edge pr
Cls prs tog
Tie a reef knot with the left pr to use for roll
T O & T B right pr and secure to work

To roll:
Use one of the Med tone threads from left edge pr from section 1 as the rolling thread
Add 1 pr Med tone threads in the same colour to start the roll
As work progresses, add 1 single thread of the lightest tone twice (see 2.35)
The roll should consist of:
1 rolling thread (Med tone)
3 roll threads (Med tone)

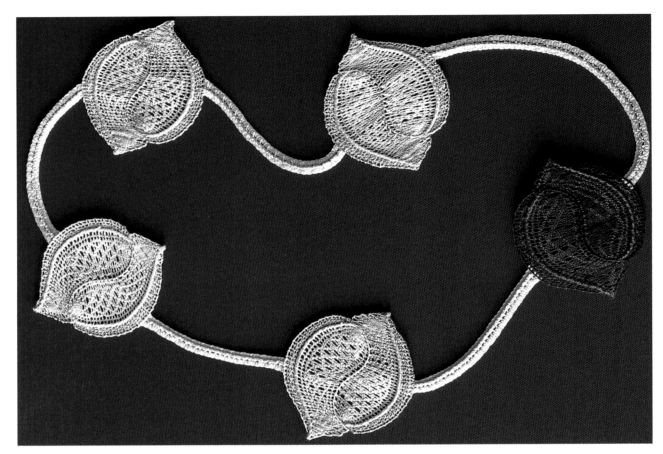

String of Pearls. Pipers Silks 80/3 and 90/3

2 roll threads (Light tone)
Towards the finish of the roll, decrease
threads singly (see 2.55)

SECTION 2

Note: Refer to colour tonal value
chart and diagram 2.66 for colours.
START at pin N# (narrow-angle

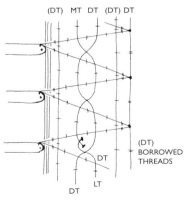

2.66 String of Pearls, pattern Ribbon sections 2 & 4

start):
Using top sewings over roll, add prs,
Cls & Tw, to centre of braid to give
order shown in diagram 2.66 (6 prs)
Change to patt Ribbon, keeping 1 pr
Cls & Tw either side of braid
Add highlights to braid thus:
Change colour of Med tone patt pr to
Light tone, in such a way as to relate
to the highlighted area of section 1
After a short distance, change the
Light tone pr back to its original tone
and colour
As braid narrows, decrease prs from
centre, change to Cls & Tw
T O & T B rem prs

SECTION 3

Note: Refer to colour tonal value
chart and diagram 2.63 for colours.

START at pin A#:
Work as section 1, using top sewings
to join to sections 1 & 2
Roll back in the same manner as
section 1

SECTION 4

Note: Refer to colour tonal value
chart and diagram 2.66 for colours.
START at pin N#:
Work as section 2, using top sewings
to join to sections 1 & 3

SECTIONS 5–20

Note: Refer to colour tonal value
chart and diagrams 2.67 & 2.68 for
colours.
Continue in the same manner as
sections 1–4, but replacing Lattice 1
with Lattice 3, variation (see 2.67)

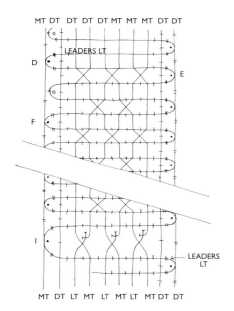

LEADERS LT

MT DT DT DT DT MT MT MT DT DT

D — E

F

I

LEADERS LT

MT DT LT MT LT MT LT MT DT DT

2.67 String of Pearls, pattern Lattice 3 (variation), for following odd-numbered sections 5–19

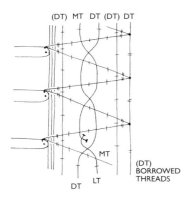

(DT) MT DT (DT) DT

MT

DT LT

(DT) BORROWED THREADS

2.68 String of Pearls, pattern Ribbon, for following even-numbered sections 6–20

Note: There is a colour change. In effect the leaders from the black pearl, sections 1–4, are a Dark tone whereas the leaders from the light pearls, sections 5–19 with odd numbers, are a Light tone (see 2.67). Sections 6–20 with even numbers are a Medium tone (see 2.68). The tonal values of the threads used for the roll are the same as used for sections 1 & 3.

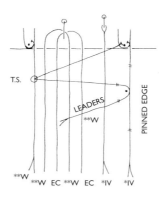

T.S.

LEADERS

**W

PINNED EDGE

**W **W EC **W EC *IV *IV

2.69 String of Pearls, start of string 1st side Tenstick

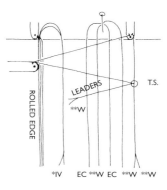

ROLLED EDGE

LEADERS

**W

T.S.

*IV EC **W EC **W **W

2.70 String of Pearls, start of string 2nd side Tenstick

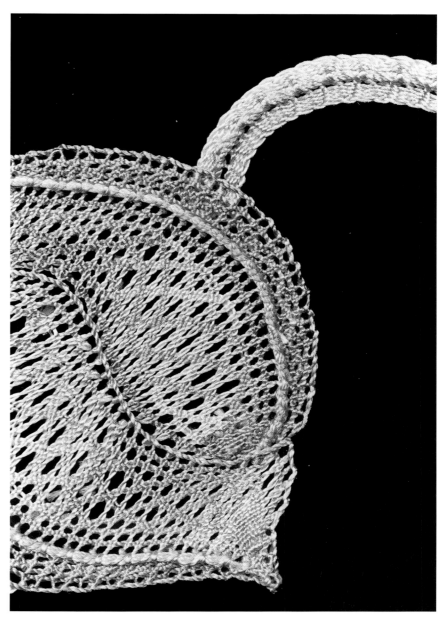

String of Pearls (detail). Rolled edge along centre of two Tenstick sections

SECTIONS 21–25

Note: Refer to diagrams 2.69 & 2.70 for colours. All sections of the string are worked identically.

START at the position indicated on the pricking (2.57 and/or 2.58) so that the pinned edge of the Tenstick will be on the right edge and the outer side of the string will be worked first (see 2.69)

Using top sewings, join 6 prs to previously worked pearl:

Hang 1 pr *IV, 1 pr EC and 1pr **W to be central passives, on temp pins, staggering the **W & EC as shown in diagram (see 2.69)

Hang on leaders **W, the smooth edge pr **W and the pinned edge pr *IV with top sewings

Cont in Tenstick to next pearl

On reaching the next pearl, work leaders to pinned edge, join in order as at beginning by sewing leaders, smooth edge pr and pinned edge pr into existing pinholes

T O all 3 prs

T O all central prs

Place 1st passive pr *IV between pinned edge pr *IV and tie a knot (these will be used for the roll)

Tie remaining prs in a bunch, using the leader pr

To roll:

Use pinned edge pr *IV and 1st passive pr *IV:

1 single rolling thread

3 threads in roll

On reaching completion of the roll, sew in prs at the base of the roll

T O & T B 1 pr, since the pinned edge pr will no longer be required, and bring across the remaining pr *IV to become 1st passive pr from the rolled edge (see 2.70)

Add prs for 2nd side of Tenstick in the same order as before, but reversed (see 2.70)

Complete 2nd side of Tenstick to match the 1st side

T O & T B prs as before

SECTIONS 25–35

Work all seven pearls first, then work all seven sections of string, working around the design in a circular order (to help maintain an even tension) as follows:

21, 22, 23, 24, 33, 34 & 35

PESCOSO

If a design is developed, an entirely different form can be created, as is shown by the motif Pescoso. Further experiments involving joining the repeated motif, including its reversal, would provide endless possibilities abounding in fish in a variety of shapes and colourways.

The previous design, String of Pearls, took account of a light source and definite, though subtle, highlights were introduced. This was achieved by changing the tonal values of the colours in use. Likewise, in this motif there is a defined light source, but the tonal change is more emphatic, because of the subject matter. In order to achieve the effect of a bright light reflecting from the scales of the fish, rather than the softer light in Fishtails and String of Pearls, more vibrant and highly contrasting colours are employed.

The choice of braids is again important in describing not only the form but also the character of the subject. A rounded form will be emphasized by the use of a braid or area of work that consists of opposing diagonal lines such as ½ stitch or any of the braids with the characteristics found in the lattice braids. Equally, the shapes formed by working Lattice 1 suggest fish scales, so the choice of Lattice 1 for the main section of braid for the body of the fish in this case is inevitable. The tail sections are worked in cloth stitch and twist in which the passive threads follow the line and the curve of the tail. The use of a subtle striped arrangement of passive threads further assists the perception of movement. The light source is again considered, and since the lower tail fin would be in shadow, it is worked with leaders of a darker tone.

The roll, which forms the spine of the fish, is one of the major design lines. It is affected by the light source as it continues right along to the tip of the tail fin. The roll is therefore allowed to be a dominant element, both in terms of increasing and diminishing thickness and the use of bright, contrasting threads.

Pricking Size: See 2.71
100%: Pipers Silks
80/3 Spun silks
*90/3 Gloss silks

Thread: Pipers (see Pricking notes) 80/3 and *90/3 are shown in the samples. See Thread notes for Crocus Leaves and Crocus.

Colours: Purple PUR
Plum PL
*Pewter *PEWT
*Mauve *MAU
*Pigeon *PIG
*Helio *HEL
Cranberry CRA

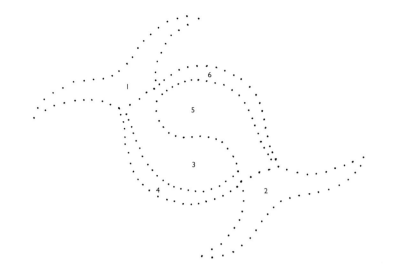

2.71 Pescoso, pricking and working order

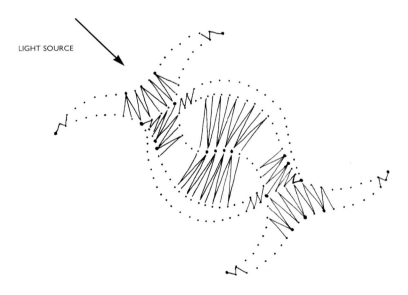

LIGHT SOURCE

2.72 Pescoso, working plan

Maroon MAR
*Coral *COR
*Marigold *MARI
*Strawberry *STR
Note: * denotes 90/3 Gloss silk; all other threads are 80/3 Spun silk.

Techniques: No (colour) change edge stitch
Two-colour point start
Magic threads

Blending colours/threads
Turning stitch
Blind pins
Changing passive patt threads
Point finish, decreasing from a wide angle
Roll (Withof)
Adding & decreasing coloured threads, roll (Withof)
Narrow-angle start
Top sewings

Stitches and Braids: Cloth stitch & twist
Cloth stitch
Lattice 1
Ribbon

To Work: Work each section numerically as shown in 2.71. See 2.72 for position of blind pins and light source. See 2.73 for start # of each section, direction of work and working direction of roll. No (colour) change edge st is used throughout. Top sewings are used throughout. Colours/threads are shown singly in thread order listings, unless otherwise indicated. Use magic threads in the same way and at the same places, where appropriate as given for Knot One, But Two.

SECTION 1
START at # (two-colour point start, see 2.72 & 2.73)
After start pin has been worked, L to R single thread order is as foll:
Left edge pr 2 x PUR
2 x PUR
2 x *PIG
Right edge pr 2 x *PIG
Leaders 2 x *PIG
Cont in Cls & Tw
adding 1 pr *MAU
1 pr *PEWT
1 pr PL (8 prs)
to give L to R single thread order as foll:
Left edge pr 2 x PUR
2 x PUR
2 x PL
2 x *PEWT
2 x *MAU
2 x *PIG
Right edge pr 2 x *PIG
Leaders 2 x *PIG (8 prs)

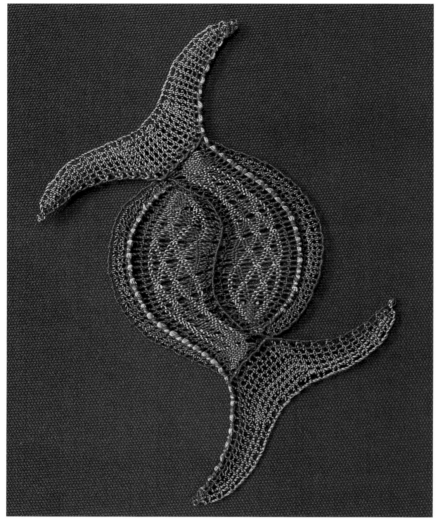

Pescoso. Pipers Silks 80/3 and 90/3

When braid reaches widest part, add 1 pr PL to become 2nd passive pr from left edge, add 1 pr *PIG to become 2nd passive pr from right edge (10 prs)
Cont in Cls & Tw to work lower part of tail fin, T O & T B prs where braid narrows, to mirror the upper part of the tail fin just worked

To finish:
T O & T B remaining prs in a bunch, secured to back of work

SECTION 2
START at # (see 2.72 & 2.73):
Work as section 1, leaders 2 x *PEWT
Note: As this tail fin is away from the light source, the leaders *PEWT are a darker tone than those used for section 1. It is possible to raise or lower the tonal value of a section of work merely by changing the leaders and leaving the passive prs unchanged.

SECTION 3
START at # (narrow-angle start, see 2.72 & 2.73):

At start pin #, hang on left edge pr CRA, and add through its loop, 2 prs Cls & Tw, left pr CRA, right pr MAR
Add leaders PUR at next pin on right side (see 2.74)
Cls & Tw to edge
Cont adding prs in Cls to centre of braid, to give order shown in diagram 2.75 (11 prs)
Cont Cls & Tw 1 pr at each side of braid
After 1st blind pin has been worked, change to patt Lattice 1 using 3 sets of 2 patt prs (see 2.75)
As work progresses, indicate highlights by changing the colour of 2 passive prs, when the prs to be changed are near the left side of the braid
Note: By counting the pinholes at the edges of the braid, it is possible to plot the course of the pattern passive threads.
Right side 2 pr patt set:
Change 1 pr PL to *STR
Middle 2 pr patt set:
Change 1 pr *COR to *MARI (see 2.64)
After a few rows (when colour change prs have crossed from one side of the braid to the other) lose the highlights by changing prs back to their original colours
Change to Cls and decrease prs when braid narrows (see 2.65)
Use right edge pr, Tw 2, to join with top sewings to left side of pinhole at base of tail fin, section 2 (this pr will be used as right edge pr for section 4) Leave
Roll back along section 3 and section 1:
Use 1 thread CRA from left edge pr as rolling thread
Add 1 pr *COR to remaining CRA

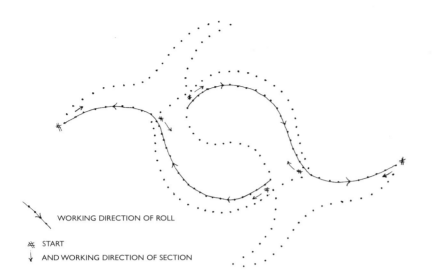

WORKING DIRECTION OF ROLL

✻ START

↓ AND WORKING DIRECTION OF SECTION

2.73 Pescoso, start and working direction, and working direction of roll

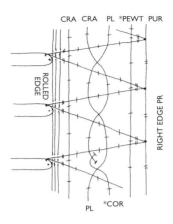

CRA CRA PL *PEWT PUR

ROLLED EDGE

RIGHT EDGE PR

PL *COR

2.76 Pescoso, sections 4 & 6, changing passive prs, pattern Ribbon

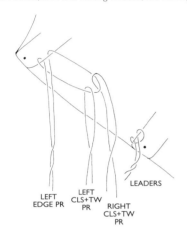

LEFT EDGE PR

LEFT CLS+TW PR

RIGHT CLS+TW PR

LEADERS

2.74 Pescoso, section 3, narrow-angle start

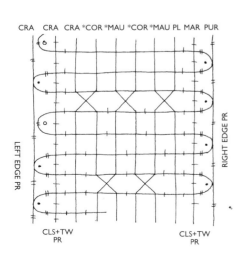

CRA CRA CRA *COR *MAU *COR *MAU PL MAR PUR

LEFT EDGE PR

RIGHT EDGE PR

CLS+TW PR

CLS+TW PR

2.75 Pescoso, sections 3 & 5, start order of pattern Lattice 1

thread from left edge pr

As roll progresses, add 4 more threads in foll order:

*STR

*MARI

*STR

*MARI

(1 rolling thread, 7 threads in roll)

Decrease threads evenly towards the finish of the roll at tip of tail fin (see 2.55)

SECTION 4 (SEE 2.72 & 2.73)

START at pin # (narrow-angle start): Cls & Tw, adding prs to give single thread order, patt Ribbon L to R as foll:

Left Cls & Tw pr 2 x CRA

2 x CRA

2 x PL

Right Cls & Tw pr 2 x *PEWT

Right edge pr 2 x PUR

Leaders 2 x *HEL (6 prs) (see 2.76)

To add highlights, change 1 pr CRA to *COR (see 2.76)

To finish, decrease prs and change to Cls & Tw when braid narrows

SECTION 5 (SEE 2.72 & 2.73)

Work as section 3

Leaders *HEL

All other colours are the same as section 3; however, as section 5 is to be joined to section 3 with top sewings, there is no left edge pr. Omit * to *. Instead, using top sewing, add 1 pr PUR to become right edge pr, section 6

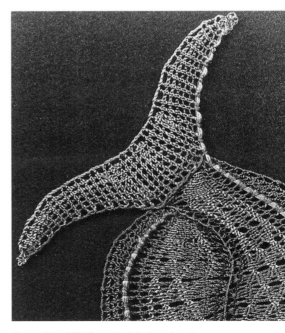

Pescoso (detail). Tail fin, and rolled edge taken along body and edge of tail

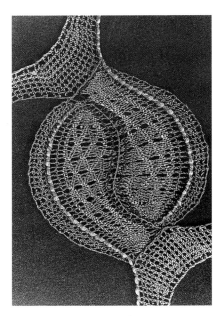

Pescoso (detail). Lattice 1 and Ribbon

Also add leaders PUR, section 6, through loop of edge pr. Leave Roll in the same way as section 3

SECTION 6 (SEE 2.72 & 2.73)

Work as section 4
Leaders PUR
All other colours are the same as section 4

CELTIC FISH

When the traditional designs in Milanese lace are studied the main characteristics are immediately apparent. The sinuous and flowing forms are rich in texture and decoration. The same description can be applied to Celtic design, hence Celtic Fish.

In Celtic Fish, the knot motif balanced opposite the point of the tail fin provides the stablizing element in a composition that suggests opposing movement within a generally symmetrical shape. It can be seen that other design elements have been employed to suggest symmetry where none exists. An ambiguity which adds visual interest is created by allowing one side of the tail fin to suggest the presence of the pelvic fin.

The convoluted spacial effects so apparent in Celtic designs are emphasized by the positioning of light against dark or colour against colour. This is achieved in Celtic Fish by using predominantly green for the fins and tail, and pink for its body. However, the greens from the dorsal fin are allowed to become one side of its body, which twists and turns in serpentine fashion, and so contrasts with the lighter, pinker side of its body.

In addition to the contrasting tonal colour values, the light source on the subject must be considered. To indicate the wetness of the fish, the changes made from light into shadow are abrupt, so the leaders and the passive pairs are frequently changed.

The scale and type of the braids chosen for this piece form important links with the areas of colour and the subject they depict. Owing to the serpentine nature of the subject, if the fish was solid, not all of its body would be viewed from the same angle, so the element of perspective must be considered for its form to be fully described. An example of this idea is when Ribbon, section 11, is used for the side of the body turning away behind at an angle, but Lattice 2, section 10, is used for the side of the body which is facing front. Similarly, Lattice 2, section 18, is used for the side of the body which is facing front, although behind Lattice 3, section 12, used for the side of the body turning forward at an angle.

The use of the rolling technique emphasizes the design line of the spine of the fish and its spacial position. The relationship of the roll to the main body of the work means that tonal values, colour vibrancy and the number of threads to be included in the roll all need careful consideration.

The roll is also used around head section 1, to draw attention to the eye of the fish, which is centrally placed to balance the design. A Milanese scroll could have been used for this section, but further emphasis of the eye is achieved by the concentric circles of colour which join to continue to describe the line of the head. The use of an open-ended start, working first one way around the circle then working the other side around to meet the first, keeps the threads in circular formation, whereas the Milanese scroll would have led to a different type of movement of thread colours.

Pricking Size: See 2.77 & 2.78
100%: Pipers Silks:
80/3 Spun silk
*90/3 Gloss silk
**300 Semi-gloss silk (white)

Thread: Pipers (see Pricking notes) 80/3, *90/3 and **300 Semi-gloss (white) silk are shown in the samples. See Thread notes for Crocus Leaves and Crocus.

Colours: **White **W
Ecru EC
Flesh FL
*Silver *SIL
Pale Lime P.LI
Pea PEA

2.77 *Celtic Fish, start, working direction, direction of roll and light source*

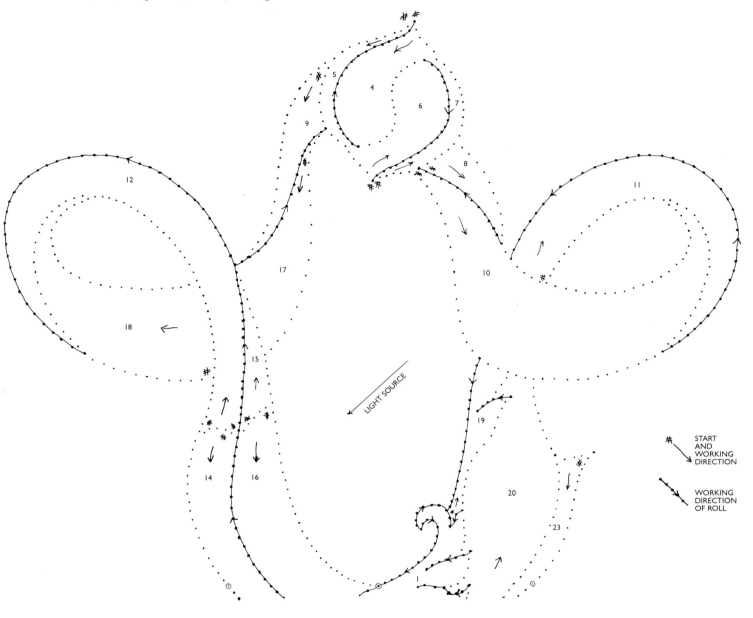

Apple APP
*Pigeon *PIG
Pewter PEW
*Mauve *MAU
Plum PL
Purple PUR
*Helio *HEL
*Pewter *PEWT
*Olive *OLI

*Seafoam *S.F.
Alice Blue AL.B
*Mint *MIN
*Water *WAT
*Sky *SKY
Note: ** denotes 300 Semi-gloss silk,
* denotes 90/3 Gloss silk; all other
threads are 80/3 Spun silk.

Techniques: No (colour) change edge
   stitch
Open-ended start
Decorative decreasing, around circle
Joining circle, keeping colours in
   position to continue
Roll, creating ribs
Locking stitch

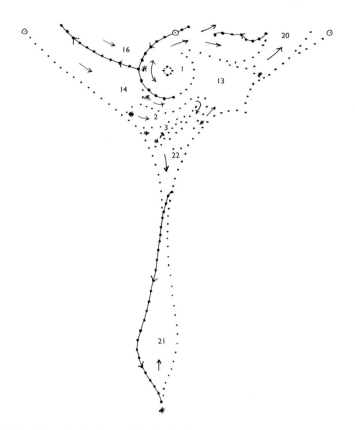

2.78 Celtic Fish, start, working direction and direction of roll

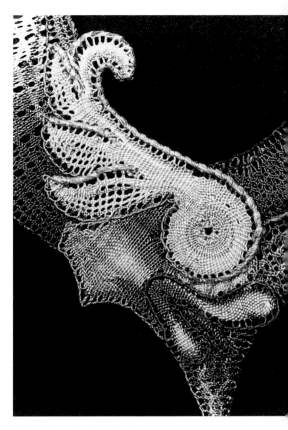

Celtic Fish: head and fins (detail)

Filling a gap, with ½ spider

One-colour round start

Tenstick colour point start

Turning stitch

Two-colour point start

Magic threads

Blending colours/threads

Blind pins

Changing passive patt threads

Changing leaders

Point finish, decreasing from a wide
    angle

Roll (Withof)

Adding & decreasing coloured
    threads, roll (Withof)

Narrow-angle start

Top sewings

Two-point start

Left: Celtic Fish. Pipers Silks 80/3 and 90/3

Stitches and Braids: Cloth stitch

Cloth stitch & twist

Tenstick

Lattice 1

Ribbon

Lattice 2

Lattice 3

To Work: The threads used to
produce the example are listed for
guidance only. The execution of the
design is entirely at the discretion of
the lacemaker. Different threads and
colours may be used, in which case
the size of the pricking may need to
be adjusted. Before commencing work,
make a second copy of the pricking
and draw in the outlines of each
section. If using different threads or
colours, also make a colour study for
reference as work progresses.

Work each section numerically as
shown in 2.77 & 2.78. See 2.77 &
2.78 for start # of each section,
direction of work, working direction
of roll and light source.

No (colour) change edge st is used
throughout. Top sewings are used
throughout. Use magic threads where
appropriate.

Although all colours used in the
example are listed at the beginning of
each section, instructions for the
colour order are not given. Expect to
change both pattern passive prs and
leaders throughout the working of this
piece.

Additional notes for techniques not
previously covered are given under
the relevant sections.

SECTION 1

Colours: **W, EC, FL, *SIL, P.LI,
PEA, APP

Stitches and Braids: Cloth stitch
Cloth stitch & twist

START at # (open-ended start):
Lay 26 prs across the pricking
vertically, securing the 13 prs at the
far side of the pillow. Leave
Note: These 13 prs will be used to
complete the second side of the circle
and will continue to work the section
after the circle is joined. These
bobbins will therefore need to be
wound more fully.
The inner circular edge must be on
the right (see 2.79 & 2.80). Note
direction of work
Work no (colour) change edge st at
pin A#, at the outer edge on the left
side
Cont in Cls
Work X T X T (Cls & Tw) with inner
circular edge pr
Note: At the inner circular edge it
will be necessary to work blind pins
(Tw 1 leaders) at the first 3 pinholes;
thereafter it will also be necessary to
decoratively decrease thus:
Work to the 4th passive pr (same
colour as leaders), Cls and return to
outer edge using 4th passive pr as
leaders (see 2.81).
Work to pin B (see 2.80 & 2.82)
Secure threads with a locking st.
Leave
Return to remaining threads hanging
at the start #
Before cont in Cls, check the edge prs
and leaders have the correct number
of twists, and adjust the tension.
Note: Leaders will be at outer edge.
Work only as far as 4th passive pr
from outer edge and, as before, Cls

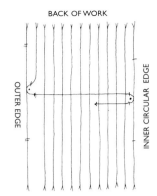

2.79 *Celtic Fish, setting up for an open-ended start*

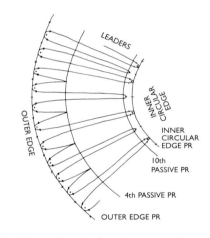

2.80 *Celtic Fish, start position and working direction*

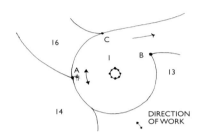

2.81 *Celtic Fish, decorative decreasing around circle*

and return to outer edge with 4th
passive pr as leaders. Work a blind pin
at inner circular edge on next row.
Cont to work around the circle,
to pin C
Secure threads with a locking st.
Leave
At the inner circular edge, start to
join circle thus:
Cls tog inner edge prs
Cls inner edge prs thro innermost

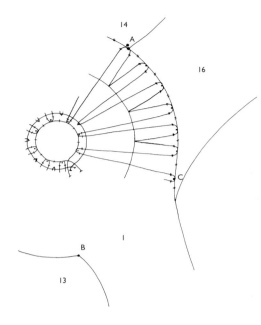

2.82 *Celtic Fish, joining circle, inner edge prs and 1st
passive prs*

passive prs, previously 10th passive prs
from outer edge
Cls tog innermost passive prs
T O & T B all 4 prs (see 2.82)
Work ½ spider with remaining 9
passive prs, from each side of circle
T O & T B 9 prs now on the right
side, i.e. towards top of the head of
fish (see 2.83)

At pin B:
Undo locking st, then edge st
Work leaders thro 1 pr passives
T O & T B leaders (see 2.83)

Return to pin C:
Undo locking st and cont in Cls with
these leaders (12 prs)
Note: When working a circle in this
way, the colours are easier to control if
the 6 central passives (passives 3–8
incl) possess similar tonal values, and
there is a passive of the same or
similar colour to the leaders as passive
no 4 from the outer edge.
The threads from the outer part of the

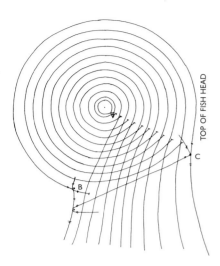

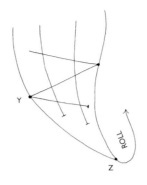

2.84 *Celtic Fish, start of roll back, 1st fin tip*

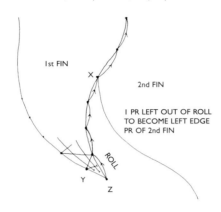

2.85 *Celtic Fish, rolling back 1st fin tip to 2nd fin tip*

2.83 *Celtic Fish, joining passive threads and continuation of braid*

circle are those which continue along the top edge of the head of the fish to the end of the section

The threads from the inner part of the circle become the lower edge of the 1st head fin

Add prs as the work widens towards the head fins

Split for the head fins thus:

Follow instructions given for Fishtails, pins D to G, working fin in Cls, using Cls & Tw for passives near left edge of fin, i.e. not the edge that will be rolled

Roll back from tip of 1st fin, creating a rib, thus:

(see Fishtails for extra rolling notes)

Work to tip, 5 prs rem (see 2.84)

After pin Y:

Cls leaders thro rem 2 passive prs

T O leaders, T O passive prs

Cls both edge prs at pin Z, placing pin Z between X T of X T X (Cls)

T O both edge prs

Place all 5 prs in a bunch to right side of fin

Use 1 thread as the rolling thread to contain the rem 9 threads in the roll

After rolling back as far as the edge of the 2nd fin, make the sewing into pin X, leaving out 1 pr Tw 2 from the roll (this pr will become the left edge pr for the 2nd fin) (see 2.85)

Cont in this way to work the remaining fins, reducing by two threads the numbers included in the roll each time

When the curled tip of the last fin is reached, add 2 prs to thicken the roll

When working the long edge of the head fin, upon reaching pin A#, decrease 1 roll thread per pin by T O with the rolling thread & T B roll thread

Note: It becomes advisable to T O the roll threads when there is a chance of

the T B threads being disturbed by continuing work, particularly when using silk.

Finish roll by making top sewing into last pinhole, T O & T B with rem thread in roll

SECTION 2

Colours: EC, FL, *SIL, P.LI, PEA, APP, *PIG, PEW, *MAU, PL

Stitches and Braids: Cloth stitch

START at # (one-colour round start): Tip of upper lip, work around section

At corner of mouth, leave out prs (incl edge pr) at 3 pinholes; bring prs back into work as the corner is rounded (see notes Morning Glory, sections 4a & 4b)

SECTION 3

Colours: *MAU, PL, PUR, *HEL

Stitches and Braids: Tenstick

START at # (Tenstick colour point start):

Tip of tongue

SECTION 4

Colours: P.LI, PEA, APP, *PIG, PEW, PL, *HEL, *PEWT, *OLI, *S.F., AL.B, *MIN, *WAT

Stitches and Braids: Cloth stitch Lattice 1 (+1 Cls & Tw pr at edges)

START at # (two-colour point start): Follow basic working instructions for String of Pearls, section 1, making the colour changes where necessary

Roll back

After completing the roll, do not cut off the threads; they are carried over to start the next section

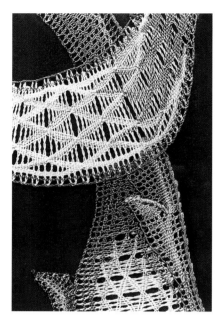

Celtic Fish (detail).

Celtic Fish (detail). Joining of braids and rolled back edges

SECTION 9

Colours: EC, *SIL, P.LI, PEA, APP, *PIG, PEW, *OLI, *S.F., *MIN, *SKY

Stitches and Braids: Ribbon (+1 Cls & Tw pr at edges)

START at # (narrow-angle start):
Roll back

SECTION 10

Colours: **W, FL, *SIL, *PIG, PEW, *MAU, PL, PUR, *HEL, *PEWT

Stitches and Braids: Lattice 2 (+1 Cls & Tw pr at edges)

START at #:
Stop work and secure bobbins in order just before the point where section 11 joins section 10
Cont by working section 11 and rolling back
Return to section 10 and complete

SECTION 5

Colours: FL, *SIL, *MAU, *HEL, *OLI

Stitches and Braids: Cloth stitch & twist
Ribbon (+1 Cls & Tw pr at right edge)

START at #:
Note: This section starts in a different place from all previous knot motifs. The threads from the roll of the previous section are not cut off; they are carried over to start this section. As braid widens, add prs to start patt
Follow the basic instructions given for String of Pearls, section 2, making the colour changes where necessary and noting that there is only one Cls & Tw pr in this section

SECTION 6

Colours: P.LI, PEA, APP, *PIG, PEW, PL, *HEL, *PEWT, *OLI, *S.F., AL.B, *MIN, *WAT

Stitches and Braids: Cloth stitch
Lattice 1 (+1 Cls & Tw pr at edges)

START at #:
See section 4

SECTION 7

Colours: *SIL, *MAU, PL, *HEL, *OLI

Stitches and Braids: Cloth stitch & twist
Ribbon (+1 Cls & Tw pr at Rt edge)

START at #:
See section 5

SECTION 8

Colours: PEA, APP, *PIG, PEW, PL, *HEL, *PEWT, *OLI, *MIN

Stitches and Braids: Ribbon (+1 Cls & Tw pr at edges)

START at #:
Roll back

SECTION 11

Colours: EC, *SIL, P.LI, PEA, APP, *PIG, PEW, *MAU, PL, *HEL, *PEWT, *OLI, *S.F., AL.B, *MIN, *WAT, *SKY

Stitches and Braids: Ribbon (+1 Cls & Tw pr at edges)

START at #:
Roll back

SECTION 12

Colours: EC, *SIL, P.LI, PEA, APP, *PIG, PEW, PL, *HEL, *PEWT, *OLI, *S.F., AL.B, *WAT

Stitches and Braids: Cloth stitch & twist
Lattice 3 (+1 Cls & Tw pr at edges)

START at # (two-point start):
For this design, work Cls & Tw, then patt when both sides have been joined

LEFT side:

Make a one-colour point start at start pin #, adding 2 passive prs on temp pin between edge prs

Cls leaders thro from outer edge to curved edge, pin and edge st

Cont adding passive prs as required

RIGHT SIDE: work to match.

When leaders reach centre pin, Cls & Tw both edge prs, pin, Cls

Work leaders thro edge prs, make T.S., and cont in patt (T O & T B central passive pr if not required) (see 2.86)

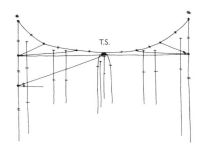

2.86 Celtic Fish, two-point start

SECTION 13

Colours: EC, FL, *SIL, P.LI, PEA, *PIG, PEW, *MAU, PL, *S.F.*MIN

Stitches and Braids: Cloth stitch

START at #:

Upper lip and work to end of mouth

Secure threads and leave

Start again at chin and work to end of mouth

T O & T B leaders, from under chin section

Cont in Cls with leaders from upper lip

At the widest point, when joining to section 1, it will be necessary to work ½ spider to fill a small gap (see 2.87)

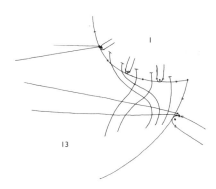

2.87 Celtic Fish, filling a gap in Cls with a ½ spider

SECTION 14

Colours: P.LI, PEA, APP, *PIG, *OLI, *MIN

Stitches and Braids: Cloth stitch & twist

Ribbon (+1 Cls & Tw pr at edges)

START at #:

Roll back to include section 12

SECTION 15

Colours: *PIG, PEW, PL, *HEL, *PEWT, *OLI

Stitches and Braids: Cloth stitch & twist

Lattice 3 (+1 Cls & Tw pr at edges)

START at # (narrow-angle start):

SECTION 16

Colours: PEA, APP, PEW, *PEWT, *OLI, *S.F

Stitches and Braids: Cloth stitch & twist

Ribbon (+1 Cls & Tw pr at edges)

START at #:

SECTION 17

Colours: *SIL, *PIG, PEW, *MAU, PL, PUR, *HEL, *PEWT

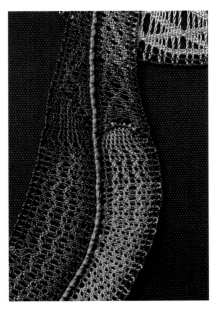

Celtic Fish (detail)

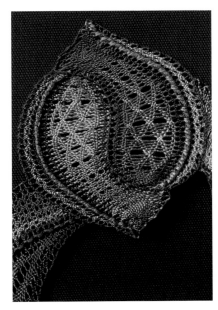

Celtic Fish (detail)

Stitches and Braids: Lattice 2 (+1 Cls & Tw pr at edges)

START at # (narrow-angle start):

Note: Make note of the thread order before top sewing into section 15, as braid continues, as if having been worked in patt, after rejoining with top sewings from section 12.

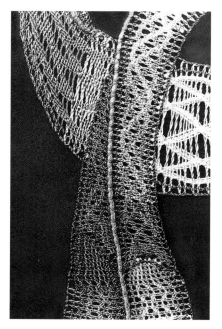

Celtic Fish (detail). Roll, crossing from centre to edge

SECTION 18

Colours: FL, *SIL, *PIG, PEW, PL, PUR, *HEL, *PEWT
Stitches and Braids: Lattice 2 (+1 Cls & Tw pr at edges)

START at #:
Cont in patt order from section 17 as if patt had been worked under the body of the fish

SECTION 19

Colours: P.LI, PEA, APP, PEW, *MIN
Stitches and Braids: Cloth stitch
Cloth stitch & twist

START at #:
Complete in same way as section 1, using Cls & Tw at the front edge of fin as before
Roll back short edge of fin, also roll along the spine of the fish

SECTION 20

Colours: FL, *SIL, *PIG, PEW, *MAU, PL, PUR, *HEL, *PEWT

Stitches and Braids: Lattice 1 (+1 Cls & Tw pr at Lt edge)

START at #:
Work patt over the top of the points of sections 1 & 13

SECTION 21

Colours: EC, P.LI, PEA, APP, PEW, *HEL, *OLI, *MIN
Stitches and Braids: Cloth stitch & twist
Ribbon (+1 Cls & Tw pr at edges)

START at # (two-colour point start):
Roll back

SECTION 22

Colours: EC, P.LI, PEA, APP, PEW, *OLI, *S.F.,*MIN
Stitches and Braids: Cloth stitch & twist
Ribbon (+1 Cls & Tw pr at edges)

START at #:
Work patt over the top of section 3 and the lower part of section 2

SECTION 23

Colours: P.LI, PEA, APP, PEW, *HEL, *OLI, *S.F., *MIN.
Stitches and Braids: Cloth stitch & twist
Ribbon (+1 Cls & Tw pr at edges)

START at # (one-colour point start)

SEA SWIRL

This design (see page 102 for illustration) won the Batsford Prize and the Simon Dukes Award at the John Bull Trophy Exhibition 1995.

A dog whelk shell found on a beach in Folkestone forms the basis for this design and relates to the cornucopia theme that frequently occurs in decorative arts from the Italian Renaissance period.

Here the theme suggests an enormous shell dredged up from the depths of the ocean spewing forth fish, seaweed and torrents of foaming water. As the contents of the shell spill out, the core of the shell is visible underneath the water, and translucent fishtails overlap one another and intermingle with seaweed.

These are interesting effects to achieve in lace. Describing the edge of the core of the shell when viewed through water requires a substantial number of very subtle colour changes and mixing of colours. Likewise, the translucent fishtails change colour but also retain their texture. The changing areas of seaweed and water provide an ambiguity which adds to the feeling of movement essential to the design.

In the same manner that the braids and their relationship with the subject have been exploited in previous designs, that relationship is again made use of here. The braids used for the water and seaweed are related and yet differ both in scale and colour. This scale is seen to be important when it is used to emphasize the shadow under the huge wave before it disperses, and shadows of fish are seen through a sheet of sunlit water.

The colours found in the shell are repeated throughout the piece as if reflecting through the water. This repetition provides essential compositional links, as found in the pinker tones of the fish that relate to the colour scheme of the shell.

Disparity is also important within the composition, and so while certain links are reinforced, others are broken. The shell only uses colours of a warm tone with cream highlights, whereas the highlights on the wet seaweed and the foam on the water are of a cold tone, namely white.

The shell, though static and performing a stabilizing function, has textural contrast to add interest: the rough exterior contrasts with the smooth interior.

It is because the shell performs such a strong role within the overall composition of the design that its contents can seem to disappear, yet without destroying the momentum created by the initial force of the water gushing out.

Pricking Size: See 2.90, 2.91, 2.92, 2.93, 2.94
100%: Gutermann Silk S 303

Thread: Gutermann Silk S 303 is shown in the sample.

Colours: 3, 5, 18, 37, 43, 50, 107, 130, 143, 158, 194, 195, 196, 213, 214, 215, 218, 309, 311, 312, 320, 339, 342, 391, 399, 423, 434, 435, 454, 472, 473, 474, 568, 585, 658, 659, 696, 703, 707, 800, 802, 810, 824, 841, 893, 915, 925

Techniques: No (colour) change edge stitch
Tenstick colour start
Mixing thread colours
Double layer Tenstick
Blind pin
Scroll (colour)
Changing leaders with passive pr
Turning stitch
One-colour point start
False picot

Rearranging threads
Changing colour of leaders
One-colour round start
Two-colour point start
Double scroll
Changing edge pr & leaders
Changing edge prs (3 variations)
Changing braid to Tenstick
Changing Tenstick to braid
Changing pinned edges of Tenstick
Tenstick colour point start
Adding & decreasing prs near edge of narrow braid
Changing Tenstick leaders
Changing/shading prs near Tenstick smooth edge
Colour shading in narrow braid
Colour shading in Tenstick
Narrow-angle start
Magic threads
Splitting braid, adding central pr & rejoining braid
Splitting braid, adding new leaders and edge prs
Working a shaped area of braid
Two-colour round start
Changing colour in pattern to introduce new colour scheme
Locking stitch
Changing edge pr with passive pr
Joining two braids tog
Joining two Tenstick braids tog
Supported Tenstick, smooth edge
Changing passive prs in patt
Two-colour point start (variation)
Creating a twisted bar for invisible sewings
Closed scroll
Top sewings
Side sewings

Stitches and Braids: Tenstick
Cloth stitch
Cloth stitch & twist
Lotus 1

Lotus 1 (variation)
Lattice 1
Lattice 3
Dewdrops
Ribbon
Lattice 2
Grenades
½ stitch

To Work: The threads used to produce the example are listed for guidance only. The execution of the design is entirely at the discretion of the lacemaker. Different threads and colours may be used, in which case the size of the pricking may need to be adjusted accordingly.

Before commencing work, make a second copy of the pricking and draw in the outlines of each section. If using different threads or colours, also make a colour study to refer to as work progresses.

Work each section numerically as in 2.90, 2.91, 2.92, 2.93 & 2.94. See 2.90–2.94 for start # of each section, direction of work and light source.

As a guide and reminder, before commencing work, scratch lines on to the pricking, to continue the outline of the shell's core. The colours are changed during the working of the sections to suggest water flowing over the shell, which is partly visible.

No (colour) change edge st is used throughout. Top sewings are used throughout unless otherwise stated. Use magic threads where appropriate.

Although all colours used in the example are listed at the beginning of each section, instructions for the colour order are not given. Expect to change both pattern passive prs and leaders throughout the working of this piece.

Sea Swirl: double Tenstick edge of shell (detail)

Additional notes for techniques not previously covered are given under the relevant sections.

SECTION 1
Colours: 3, 5, 50, 215, 320 & 802
Stitches and Braids: Tenstick

SECTION 2
Colours: 3, 5, 50, 215, 320, 473, 474 & 802
Stitches and Braids: Tenstick
Note: Section 2 Tenstick is much wider than the Tenstick of section 1. It is worked over the top of section 1, joined by top sewings.

SECTIONS 3–9
Colours: 3, 5, 50, 130, 215, 320, 423, 454, 473, 474, 696 & 802
Stitches and Braids: Cloth stitch & twist
Lotus 1

Note: All these sections are worked in the same manner. Sections 3–7, which

need to be joined to sections 1 & 2, are sewn in, then when the last pr is tied off, it is twisted several times, then sewn in once again and tied at short intervals along the length of sections 1 & 2 to create a series of twisted bars. These bars can then be used by other braids with contrasting or undesirable threads where they may be joined invisibly. This method may also be used to avoid making numerous sewings into one bar when one section is worked over by another and the finish of the last section worked will be hidden behind the first section worked. Care must be taken with tension when making the sewings or the twisted bar will be pulled into view (see 2.88).

SECTION 10
Colours: 18, 107, 130, 194, 214, 218, 309, 339, 342, 399, 472, 585, 696, 707, 800, 841, 915 & 925
Stitches and Braids: Cloth stitch
Lattice 1

SECTION 11 & 12
Colours: 5, 18, 37, 107, 130, 143, 194, 195, 196, 214, 218, 312, 309, 339, 342, 391, 435, 472, 707, 800, 824, 915 & 925
Stitches and Braids: Cloth stitch
Lattice 3

Note: Colours change over shell.

Sea Swirl (detail). Seaweed, water and fishtails flowing over core of shell

SECTIONS 13, 13A & 22
Colours: 5, 50, 215, 320, 423, 454, 473, 474 & 802
Stitches and Braids: Cloth stitch

SECTION 14
Colours: 5, 130, 215, 320, 423, 454, 473 & 474
Stitches and Braids: Cloth stitch

SECTION 15
Colours: 5, 37, 43, 50, 143, 158, 194, 195, 320, 435, 473, 474, 568, 659, 800 & 802
Stitches and Braids: Cloth stitch
Dewdrops
Cloth stitch & twist
Ribbon

Splitting braid to work body of fish thus (see also 2.28):
Work to left edge, leave leaders
Add central edge pr over pin, Cls with central passive pr, place pin after X T of X T X

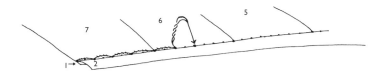

2.88 Sea Swirl, creating a twisted bar for invisible sewings

Central passive pr have now become leaders

Tw 2 both prs and cont with right side of fish

Return to work left side using leaders left at pin, top sewing into central edge

To rejoin braid:

Work leaders from edges back to centre, make T.S.:

either leave the new central passives to cont in braid

or T O & T B if the colours are unsuitable (see 2.89)

Colours change where fishtail crosses over other fishtail and shell

Sea Swirl (detail). Double Tenstick edge of shell, also Lotus I

SECTION 16

Colours: 5, 18, 37, 50, 107, 158, 195, 320, 568, 802 & 915

Stitches and Braids: Cloth stitch
Dewdrops
Ribbon

Note: See section 15.

SECTION 17

Colours: 5, 18, 37, 50, 107, 143, 158, 568 & 915

Stitches and Braids: Cloth stitch
Dewdrops
Cloth stitch & twist

Note: See section 15.

SECTION 18

Colours: 5, 18, 37, 143, 158, 435 & 568

Stitches and Braids: Cloth stitch
Dewdrops

Note: See section 15.

SECTION 19

Colours: 5, 18, 158, 435, 568 & 915

Stitches and Braids: Cloth stitch
Dewdrops

Note: See section 15.

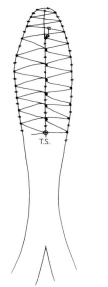

2.89 Sea Swirl, splitting braid for fish and adding central pr, rejoining braid

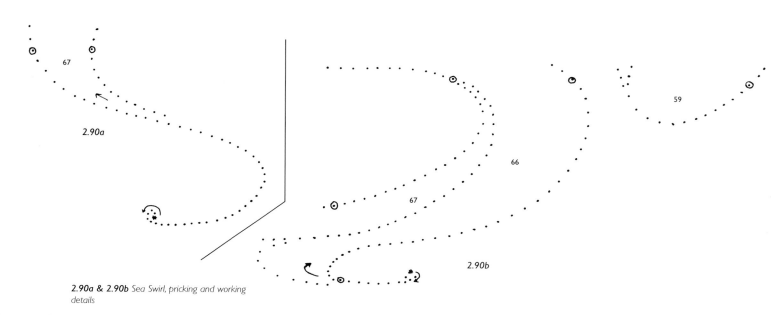

2.90a & 2.90b Sea Swirl, pricking and working details

95

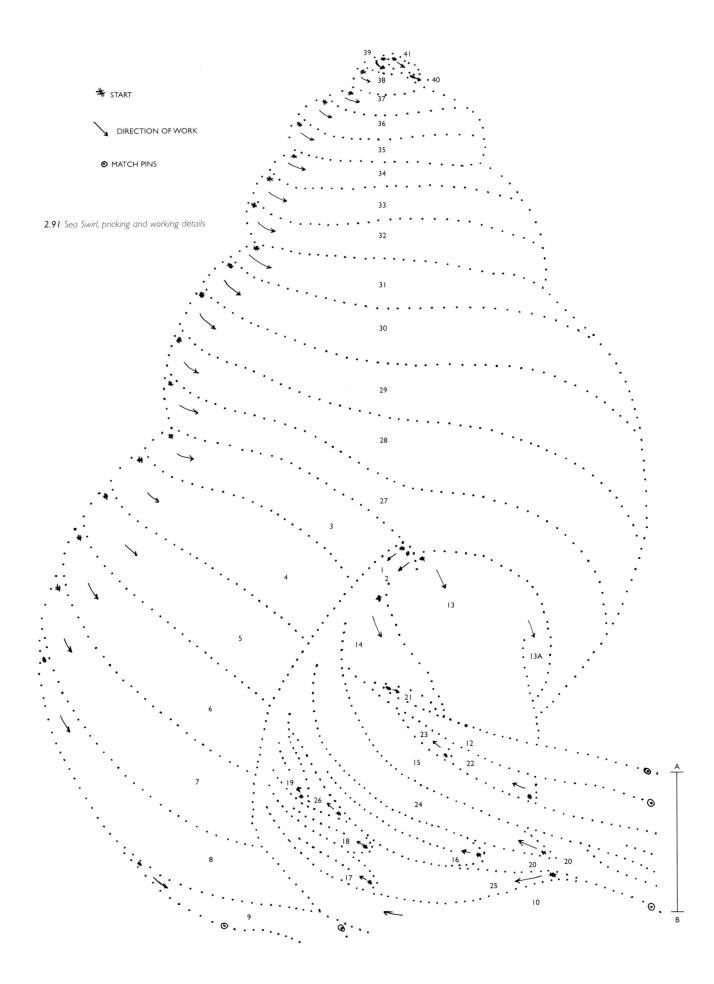

2.91 Sea Swirl, pricking and working details

✳ START

↘ DIRECTION OF WORK

⊙ MATCH PINS

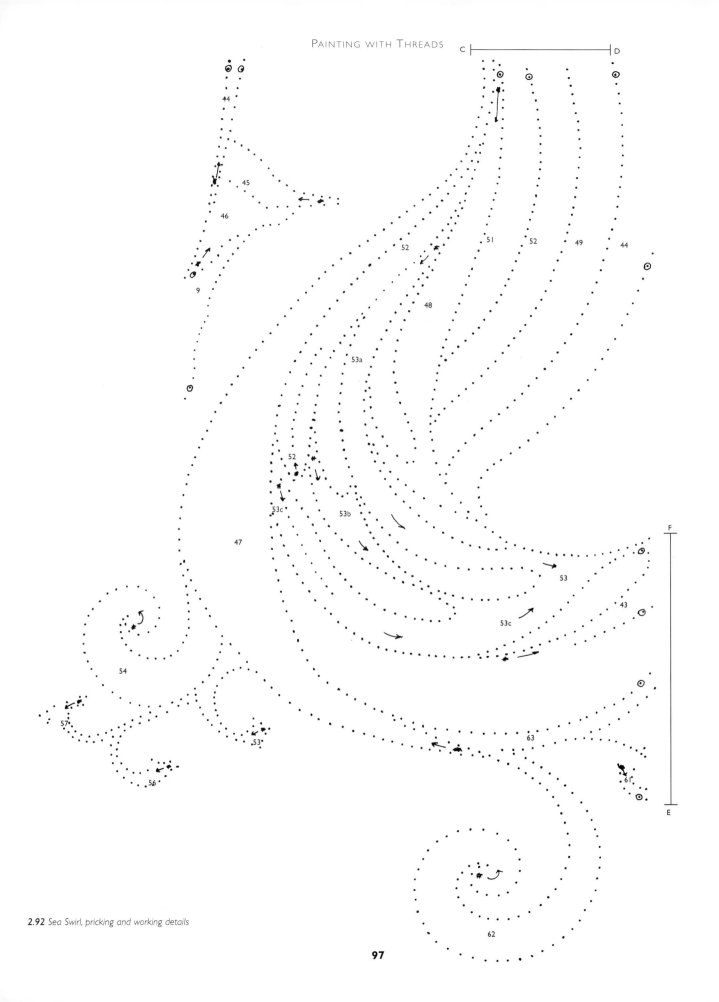

2.92 Sea Swirl, pricking and working details

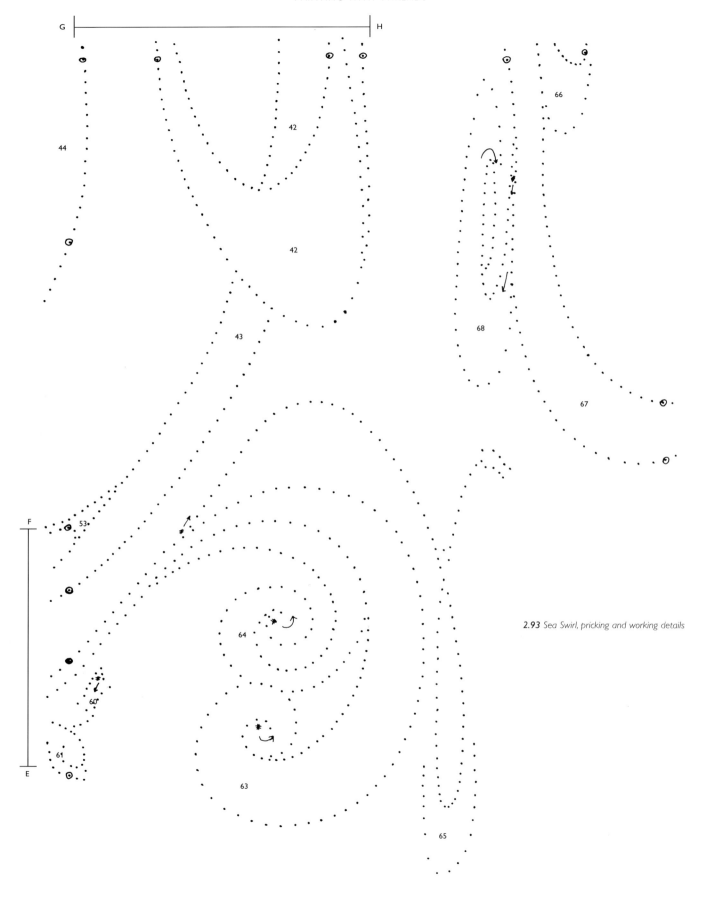

2.93 Sea Swirl, pricking and working details

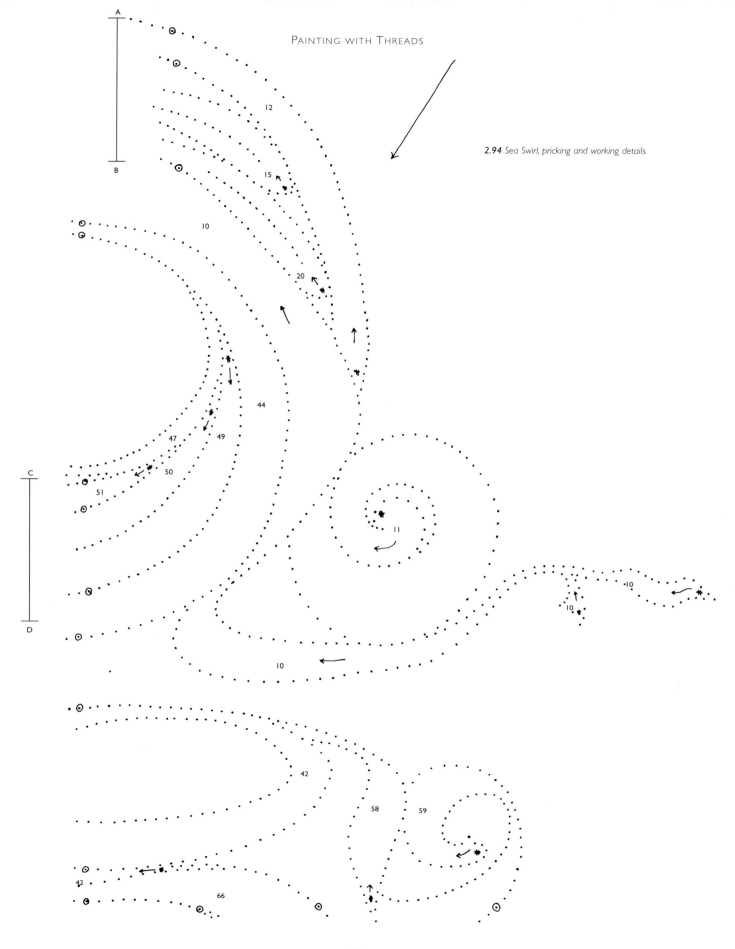

2.94 Sea Swirl, pricking and working details

SECTION 20
Colours: 5, 37, 43, 50, 143, 158, 194, 195, 320, 435, 454, 473, 474, 568, 658, 659, 800, 802 & 893
Stitches and Braids: Cloth stitch
Dewdrops
Cloth stitch & twist
Ribbon

Note: See section 15. After rejoining braid to work the remaining part of the body of the fish, the braid is split again in a different way (see Fishtails, 2.41). New leaders and edge prs are added. Colours change over shell. Side sewings into section 15.

SECTION 21
Colours: 130 & 696
Stitches and Braids: Cloth stitch

SECTION 22
See section 13.

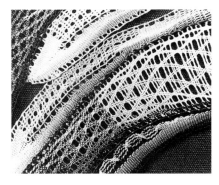

Sea Swirl (detail). Fish amongst seaweed

SECTION 23
Colours: 130, 423 & 474
Stitches and Braids: Cloth stitch

SECTION 24
Colours: 5, 37, 143, 158, 194, 195, 196, 309, 311, 312, 320, 339, 435, 473, 474, 824 & 893
Stitches and Braids: Cloth stitch

Note: Colours change over shell. Side sewings into section 15.

SECTION 25
Colours: 5, 37, 143, 158, 194, 195, 196, 309, 311, 312, 320, 339, 435, 473, 474, 568, 824 & 893
Stitches and Braids: Cloth stitch

Note: Colours change over shell.

SECTION 26
Colours: 309, 312 & 339
Stitches and Braids: Cloth stitch

SECTION 27
Colours: 5, 50, 130, 215, 320, 423, 454, 473, 474, 696 & 802
Stitches and Braids: Cloth stitch & twist
Lotus 1

Note: Side sewings into sections 3 & 13.

SECTIONS 28–30
Colours: 3, 5, 50, 130, 215, 320, 423, 454, 473, 474, 696 & 802
Stitches and Braids: Cloth stitch & twist
Lotus 1

SECTION 31
Colours: 5, 50, 130, 215, 320, 423, 454, 473, 474, 696 & 802
Stitches and Braids: Cloth stitch & twist
Lotus 1

SECTION 32
Colours: 5, 130, 215, 320, 423, 454, 473, 474, 696 & 802
Stitches and Braids: Cloth stitch & twist
Lotus 1

Note: Side sewings into section 31.

SECTION 33
Colours: 3, 5, 50, 130, 215, 320, 423, 454, 473, 474, 696 & 802
Stitches and Braids: Cloth stitch & twist
Note: Lotus 1

SECTION 34
Colours: 5, 50, 130, 215, 320, 423, 454, 473, 474, 696 & 802
Stitches and Braids: Cloth stitch & twist
Lotus 1 (var)

Note: Lotus 1, variation with 4 passive prs, thus:
*Cls Lt pr tog
Cls Rt pr tog
Cls centre prs tog*
Rep * to *
Cls leaders thro 2 prs,
Tw 2 leaders,
Cls rem 2 prs & cont

SECTION 35
Colours: 5, 130, 215, 320, 423, 454, 473, 474, 696 & 802
Stitches and Braids: Cloth stitch & twist
Lotus 1 (var)

Note: See section 34 for Lotus 1, variation. Side sewings into section 34.

SECTION 36
Colours: 3, 5, 50, 130, 215, 320, 423, 454, 473, 474 and 696
Stitches and Braids: Cloth stitch & twist
Lotus 1 (var)

Note: See section 34 for Lotus 1, variation.

SECTION 37
Colours: 5, 130, 215, 423, 454, 473, 474 & 696
Stitches and Braids: Cloth stitch & twist
Lotus 1 (var)

Note: See section 34 for Lotus 1, variation.

SECTION 38
Colours: 130, 215, 320, 423, 454, 473, 474 & 696
Stitches and Braids: Cloth stitch & twist
Lotus 1 (var)

Note: See section 34 for Lotus 1, variation. Side sewings into section 37.

SECTION 39
Colours: 320, 454, 473 & 696
Stitches and Braids: Cloth stitch & twist

SECTION 40
Colours: 423, 454, 474 & 696
Stitches and Braids: Cloth stitch & twist

SECTION 41
Colours: 130, 423, 474 & 696
Stitches and Braids: Cloth stitch & twist

SECTION 42
Colours: 18, 37, 107, 130, 143, 194, 195, 196, 213, 218, 309, 339, 342, 707, 800, 841, 915 & 925
Stitches and Braids: Cloth stitch
Lattice 2
Lattice 1

SECTION 43
Colours: 18, 107, 130, 194, 195, 309, 339, 342, 707, 800, 841, 915 & 925
Stitches and Braids: Lattice 1
Tenstick

SECTION 44
Colours: 143, 213, 214, 218, 309, 311, 312, 339 & 800
Stitches and Braids: Cloth stitch
Grenades
Tenstick

SECTION 45
Colours: 5, 50, 215, 320, 473 & 802
Stitches and Braids: Cloth stitch

SECTION 46
Colours: 50, 130, 158, 215, 320, 423, 454, 473, 474, 568 & 696
Stitches and Braids: Cloth stitch

SECTION 47
Colours: 18, 194, 309, 342, 399, 472, 585, 707, 800, 824, 841 & 915
Stitches and Braids: Cloth stitch
Lattice 1

SECTION 48
Colours: 194 & 800
Stitches and Braids: ½ stitch (+ 1 pr Cls, as 1st passive pr at edges)

SECTION 49
Colours: 143, 213, 214, 309, 311, 312 & 339
Stitches and Braids: Dewdrops

Note: Side sewings into section 44.

SECTION 50
Colours: 143, 213, 214, 218, 309, 311, 312 & 339
Stitches and Braids: Ribbon
Note: Side sewings into section 49.

SECTION 51
Colours: 214, 309, 312 & 339
Stitches and Braids: Ribbon

Note: Side sewings into section 50.

SECTION 52
Colours: 194, 311, 703, 800, 824 & 925
Stitches and Braids: ½ stitch (+ 1 pr Cls, as 1st passive pr at edges)

SECTION 53A
Colours: 194, 311, 703, 800, 824 & 925
Stitches and Braids: ½ stitch (+ 1 pr Cls, as 1 st passive pr at edges)

SECTION 53B
Colours: 194, 800 & 824
Stitches and Braids: ½ stitch (+ 1 pr Cls, as 1st passive pr at edges)

SECTION 53C
Colours: 194, 800, 824, 915 & 925
Stitches and Braids: ½ stitch (+ 1 pr Cls, as 1st passive pr at edges)

SECTION 54
Colours: 18, 107, 130, 194, 309, 342, 707, 800, 824, 841, 915 & 925
Stitches and Braids: Cloth stitch
Lattice 3

SECTION 55
Colours: 18, 130, 309, 342, 585, 707 & 841
Stitches and Braids: ½ stitch
Cloth stitch

SECTIONS 56 & 57
Colours: 18, 309, 342, 707, 800, 915 & 925
Stitches and Braids: Cloth stitch

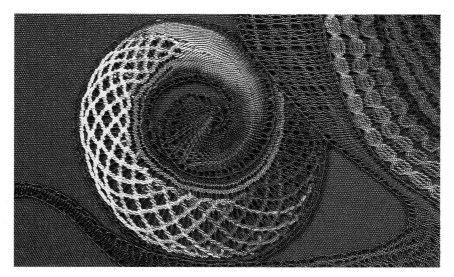

Sea Swirl: scroll (detail)

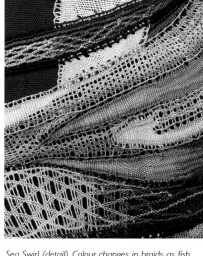

Sea Swirl (detail). Colour changes in braids as fish and water flow over core of shell, allowing shape of shell to show through

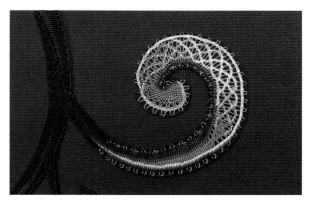

Sea Swirl (detail). Highlights Lattice 3

Sea Swirl (detail). Shadow of wave and invisible fish in ½ st water

Sea Swirl: fish, seaweed and wave (detail)

Left: Sea Swirl. Gutermann Silk S 303

SECTION 58
Colours: 309, 339, 342, 585, 707 &
841
Stitches and Braids: Cloth stitch
Lattice 1

SECTION 59
Colours: 18, 130, 309, 339, 342, 399,
585, 707, 800 & 841
Stitches and Braids: Cloth stitch
Lattice 1

SECTIONS 60 & 61
Colours: 18, 309, 342, 707, 800, 841,
915 & 925
Stitches and Braids: Cloth stitch
Tenstick

SECTION 62
Colours: 18, 194, 339, 800, 824, 915
& 925
Stitches and Braids: Cloth stitch
Lattice 3

SECTION 63
Colours: 18, 130, 309 ,312, 339, 342,
399, 585, 707, 800, 824, 841 & 915
Stitches and Braids: Cloth stitch
Lattice 2

Note: See 2.95, 2.96 and also 1.42.
The closed scroll is worked normally
as a Milanese (colour) scroll, but the
inner edge pr is included in the work
as a passive pr, or T O & T B, while
the top sewings are made into the
previously worked scroll section.
When pin X (2.96) is reached, the
passive pr may become the inner edge
pr again, or if a different colour is
required a new pr can be added.

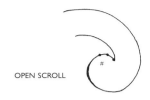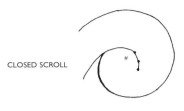

2.95 Sea Swirl, examples of open and closed scrolls

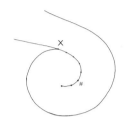

2.96 Sea Swirl, closed scroll

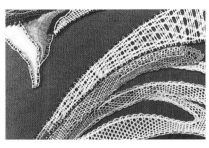

Sea Swirl (detail). Base of shell, also top of wave
with invisible fish

SECTION 64
Colours: 18, 143, 194, 196, 213, 218,
309, 311, 312, 339, 342, 435, 707,
800, 824, 915 & 925
Stitches and Braids: Cloth stitch
Lattice 3

SECTION 65
Colours: 18, 143, 194, 196, 218, 309,
311, 312, 339, 342, 585, 707, 800, 824
& 841
Stitches and Braids: Tenstick
Cloth stitch
Lattice 1

SECTION 66
Colours: 143, 213, 309, 339 & 800
Stitches and Braids: Tenstick
Cloth stitch
Lattice 2

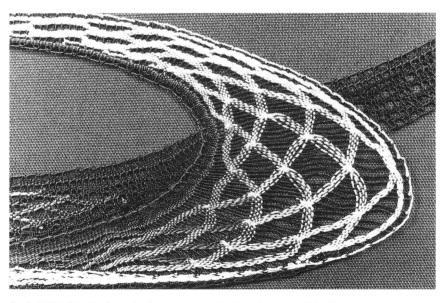

Sea Swirl (detail). Lattice 2 imitating foam on water; note extra twists made with leaders

Sea Swirl (detail). Highlights on seaweed, Lattice 3

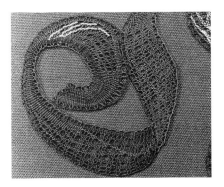

Sea Swirl (detail). Highlights and shadow worked with Lattice 1

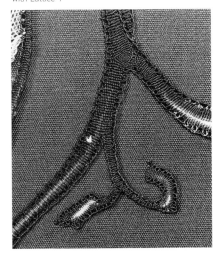

Sea Swirl (detail). Joining two braids together

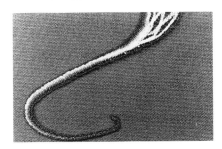

Sea Swirl (detail). Changing pinned edge braid to Tenstick

Sea Swirl (detail). Closed scroll, Braids: Lattice 2 and 3

SECTION 67

Colours: 143, 213, 218, 309, 339 & 800

Stitches and Braids: Tenstick
Cloth stitch
Lattice 2

SECTION 68

Colours: 18, 194, 309, 339, 342, 707, 841 & 925

Stitches and Braids: Cloth stitch
Lattice 1

ON REFLECTION

Mirror images can frequently produce fascinating shapes and tensions within a design, but there is always a risk of predictability and monotony. Merely reflecting the shell and some of the torrent from Sea Swirl would produce a pleasing though not particularly interesting centre shape, and a design without narrative substance.

When the torrent is redrawn with the addition of a fantastic dolphin, of the Renaissance style and colouring, with extra scrolls and seaweed, the design is immediately livelier and more interesting.

The central shape is broken by the curl of the dolphin's head fin. The shape of this curl and the other fins is repeated in the additional seaweed shapes below, which continue the Renaissance theme.

The very dark blues found in the lower central sections balance the blues where the torrent gushes out of the shell; likewise the greens of the dolphin relate to those of the seaweed.

By placing the shells so that they are only just touching end to end, an unusual tension is created. The shells appear to spin away, as if suspended, whereas the force of the torrent is pulling them forward, so an uneasy balance is formed which gives the illusion of movement. This balance is further strengthened by positioning the eye of the dolphin directly under the centre of the joined shells.

The introductory notes for Sea Swirl also apply to On Reflection. However, there are differences in working this design, mainly in the use of rolled edges. Instead of the double layer of Tenstick for the edge of the shell, one layer of Tenstick and a rolled edge are used. Rolled edges are also used on some of the sections of seaweed and there are two rolled scrolls. The dolphin has rolled edges in exactly the same way as those found in Celtic Fish.

In this design the dolphin is worked in exactly the same way as Celtic Fish, although using different colours. The dolphin's head, main body and tail sections use exactly the same pricking and braids as those for Celtic Fish.

The light source, when working the design, travels from right to left at an angle. Hence the shells are not worked identically; their highlights and shadows are in completely different areas. Likewise, the mirror image fish are lit from one side, so special consideration must be given when working the overlapping, translucent tailfins.

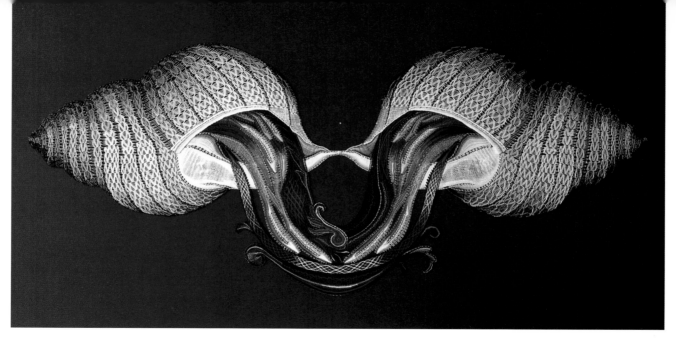

On Reflection. Gutermann Silk S 303

On Reflection (detail): dolphin's head and tail fin, fish and seaweed. Shadows on fish

Pricking Size: See 2.97, 2.98, 2.99 & 2.100
100%: Gutermann Silk S 303

Thread: Gutermann Silk S 303 is shown in the sample.

Colours: 3, 5, 18, 23, 37, 50, 130, 143, 158, 194, 195, 213, 214, 215, 218, 237, 283, 309, 311, 312, 320, 336, 339, 342, 391, 402, 423, 435, 454, 473, 474, 482, 483, 553, 568, 580, 582, 585, 658, 696, 707, 722, 800, 802, 810, 824, 835, 841, 869, 870, 893, 904 & 965

Techniques: No (colour) change edge stitch
Tenstick colour start
Mixing thread colours
Roll (Withof)
Adding & decreasing prs from roll
Blind pin
Open-ended start
Decorative decreasing around circle
Joining circle, keeping colours in position to continue
Roll, creating ribs
Working over Tenstick
Filling a gap with ½ spider
Changing leaders with passive pr
Turning stitch
One-colour point start
False picot
Rearranging threads
Changing colour of leaders
One-colour round start
Two-colour point start
Scroll (colour)
Closed scroll
Rolled scroll in colour

Changing edge pr & leaders
Changing edge prs (3 variations)
Tenstick colour point start
Adding & decreasing prs near edge of narrow braid
Colour shading in narrow braid
Colour shading in Tenstick
Narrow-angle start
Magic threads
Splitting braid, adding central pr & rejoining braid
Splitting braid, adding new leaders & edge prs
Working a shaped area of braid
Two-colour round start
Changing colour in pattern to introduce new colour scheme
Locking stitch
Changing edge pr with passive pr
Joining two braids together
Changing passive prs in patt
Two-colour point start (variation)
Creating a twisted bar for invisible sewings
Top sewings
Side sewings

Stitches and Braids: Tenstick
Cloth stitch

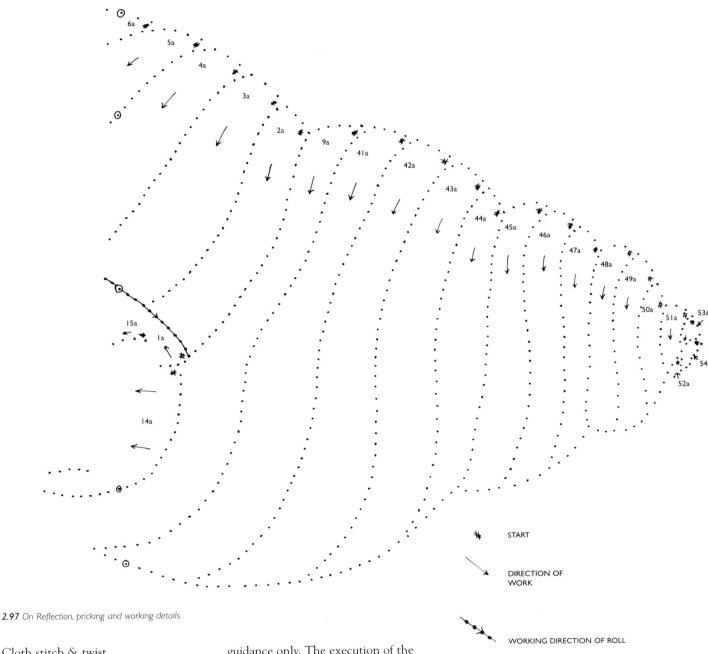

2.97 On Reflection, pricking and working details

Cloth stitch & twist
Lotus 1
Lotus 1 (variation)
Lattice 3
Dewdrops
Ribbon
Lattice 1

To Work: The threads used to produce the example are listed for guidance only. The execution of the design is entirely at the discretion of the lacemaker. Different threads and colours may be used, in which case the size of the pricking may need to be adjusted accordingly.

Before commencing work, make a second copy of the pricking and draw in the outlines of each section. If you are using different threads or colours,

it is also a good idea to make a colour study to refer to as the work progresses.

Work each section numerically as shown in 2.97, 2.98, 2.99 & 2.100. See 2.97–2.100 for start # of each section, direction of work and light source.

START
DIRECTION OF WORK
WORKING DIRECTION OF ROLL

As a guide and reminder, before commencing work, scratch lines on to the pricking to continue the outline of the shell's core. The colours are changed during the working of the sections to suggest water flowing over the shell, which is partly visible.

No (colour) change edge st is used throughout. Top sewings are used throughout unless otherwise stated. Use magic threads where appropriate.

Although all colours used are listed at the beginning of each section, instructions for the colour order are not given. Expect to change both pattern passive prs and leaders throughout the working of this piece.

Additional notes for techniques not previously covered are given under the relevant sections.

SECTIONS 1 & 1A
Colours: 3, 5, 50, 215, 320, 473, 474 & 802

Stitches and Braids: Tenstick

Note: Roll back.

SECTIONS 2 & 2A
Colours: < 2 > 5, 23, 50, 130, 320, 339, 423, 454, 473, 474, 696, 722 & 893
< 2a > omit 23 & 50
Stitches and Braids: Cloth stitch & twist
Lotus 1

Note: Make twisted bar, see Sea Swirl, sections 3–7, notes.

SECTIONS 3 & 3A
Colours: < 3 > 5, 23, 50, 130, 215, 320, 423, 454, 473, 474, 696, 722, 802 & 893
< 3a > Omit 23
Stitches and Braids: Cloth stitch & twist
Lotus 1

Note: Make twisted bar.

SECTIONS 4 & 4A
Colours: 3, 5, 23, 50, 130, 215, 320, 423, 454, 473, 474, 696, 722, 802 & 893
Stitches and Braids: Cloth stitch & twist
Lotus 1

Note: Make twisted bar.

SECTIONS 5 & 5A
Colours: 3, 5, 23, 50, 130, 215, 320, 423, 454, 473, 474, 696, 722, 802 & 893
Stitches and Braids: Cloth stitch & twist
Lotus 1

Note: Make twisted bar.

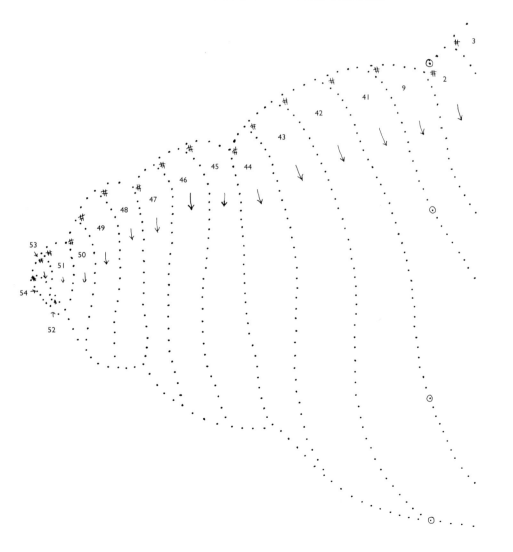

2.98 On Reflection, pricking and working details

SECTIONS 6 & 6A

Colours: 3, 5, 23, 50, 130, 215, 320, 423, 454, 473, 474, 696, 722, 802 & 893

Stitches and Braids: Cloth stitch & twist

Lotus 1

Note: Make twisted bar.

SECTIONS 7 & 7A

Colours: 3, 5, 23, 50, 130, 215, 320, 423, 454, 473, 474, 696, 722, 802 & 893

Stitches and Braids: Cloth stitch & twist

Lotus 1

Note: Roll back.

SECTIONS 8 & 8A

Colours: < 8 > 5, 23, 50, 130, 320, 423, 454, 473, 474, 696, 802 & 893
< 8a > add 3, 215 & 722

Stitches and Braids: Cloth stitch & twist

Lotus 1

Note: Roll back.

SECTIONS 9 & 9A

Colours: < 9 > 3, 5, 23, 50, 130, 215, 320, 339, 423, 454, 473, 474, 696, 722, 802 & 893
< 9a > Omit 339

Note: Side sewings into sections 2 & 2a.

SECTION 10

Colours: 3, 18, 237, 402, 483, 580, 582, 585, 835, 841 & 870

Stitches and Braids: Cloth stitch

Note: Roll back along fins, creating ribs, and also back along top of head of dolphin (see diagrams 2.79–2.85).

SECTION 11

Colours: 3, 18, 582, 585, 841 & 893

Stitches and Braids: Cloth stitch

SECTION 12

Colours: 18, 582 & 870

Stitches and Braids: Tenstick

SECTIONS 13 & 13A

Colours: 3, 18, 37, 158, 194, 195, 213, 218, 283, 309, 311, 312, 336, 339, 435, 553, 580, 582, 585, 800, 802, 824, 835, 841, 869 & 904

Stitches and Braids: Cloth stitch
Lattice 3 (+1 pr Cls, to be passives at edges)

SECTIONS 14 & 14A

Colours: 5, 50, 215, 320, 423, 454, 473, 474 & 802

Stitches and Braids: Cloth stitch

Note: Use side sewings to hang on passive prs from section 9.

SECTIONS 15 & 15A

Colours: 5, 130, 215, 320, 423, 454, 473 & 474

Stitches and Braids: Cloth stitch

SECTIONS 16 & 16A

Colours: 5, 37, 143, 158, 194, 283, 311, 320, 391, 435, 473, 474, 568, 553, 658, 800 & 869

Stitches and Braids: Cloth stitch
Dewdrops
Cloth stitch & twist
Ribbon

Note: Colours change where fishtail crosses over other fishtail and shell.

SECTIONS 17 & 17A

Colours: 37, 158, 194, 283, 311, 320, 435, 553, 568, 802 & 869

Stitches and Braids: Cloth stitch
Dewdrops
Cloth stitch & twist
Ribbon

SECTIONS 18 & 18A

Colours: 37, 143, 158, 194, 283, 311, 320, 553, 568, 585, 800 & 869

Stitches and Braids: Cloth stitch
Dewdrops
Cloth stitch & twist
Ribbon

Notes: Colours change over shell.
Side sewings into sections 16 & 16a.

SECTION 19

Colours: 18, 283, 482, 483, 585, 835 & 870

Stitches and Braids: Cloth stitch

Note: See 2.87.

SECTION 20

Colours: 18, 237, 283, 342, 399, 582, 585, 707, 835, 841, 869 & 904

Stitches and Braids: Cloth stitch
Cloth stitch & twist

Note: Roll back along fins, creating ribs, and also back along spine of dolphin.

SECTION 21

Colours: 18, 237, 482, 483, 834, 841 & 870

Stitches and Braids: Lattice 1

Note: Work over tips of fins from sections 10, 19 & 20.

SECTION 22

Colours: 18, 237, 482, 483, 841 & 870

Stitches and Braids: Lattice 1

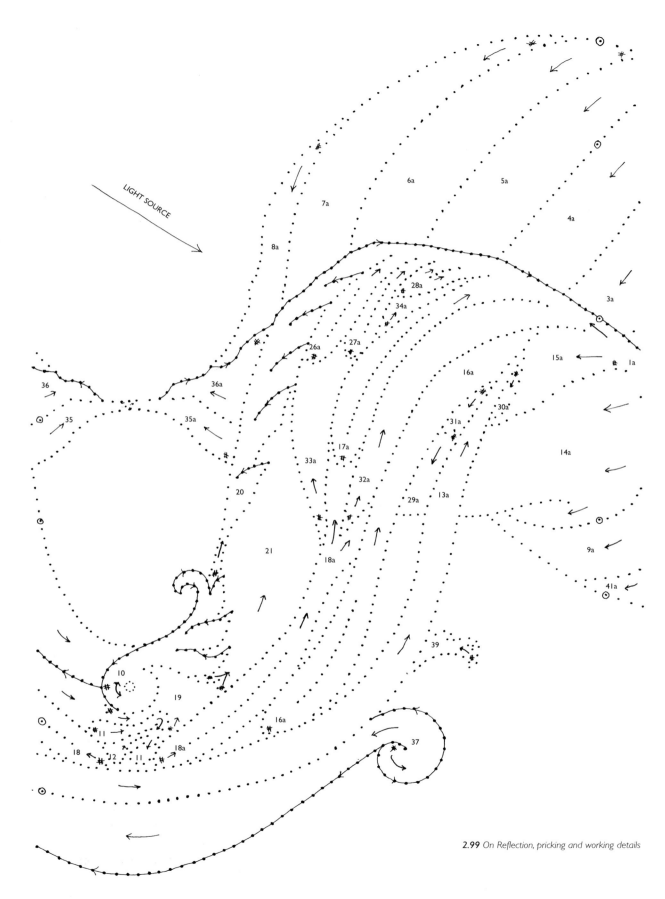

LIGHT SOURCE

2.99 On Reflection, pricking and working details

2.100 On Reflection, pricking and working details

SECTION 23

Colours: 18, 283, 342, 399, 582, 585, 835 & 841

Stitches and Braids: Cloth stitch & twist

Ribbon

Note: Roll back to include section 22.

SECTION 24

Colours: 18, 342, 707, 841, 870 & 904

Stitches and Braids: Lattice 1

SECTION 25

Colours: 18, 342, 399, 585, 707, 835 & 841

Stitches and Braids: Cloth stitch & twist

Ribbon

SECTIONS 26 & 26A

Colours: 37, 158, 195, 311, 320, 553, 568 & 869

Stitches and Braids: Cloth stitch

Dewdrops

Cloth stitch & twist

SECTIONS 27 & 27A

Colours: 37, 196, 158, 214, 311, 342, 568 & 869

Stitches and Braids: Cloth stitch

Dewdrops

Cloth stitch & twist

SECTIONS 28 & 28A

Colours: 18, 37, 158, 214, 311, 312 & 342

Stitches and Braids: Cloth stitch

Dewdrops

Cloth stitch & twist

SECTIONS 29 & 29A

Colours: 5, 50 & 802

Stitches and Braids: Cloth stitch

SECTIONS 30 & 30A

Colours: 130, 423 & 696

Stitches and Braids: Cloth stitch

SECTIONS 31 & 31A

Colours: 130, 423 & 474

Stitches and Braids: Cloth stitch

SECTIONS 32 & 32A

Colours: 5, 18, 37, 158, 214, 218, 309, 311, 312, 320, 339, 391, 435, 473, 474, 553, 568, 707, 810, 824, 869, 904 & 965

Stitches and Braids: Cloth stitch

Note: Colour change over shell.

SECTIONS 33 & 33A

Colours: 3, 5, 18, 37, 158, 214, 218, 309, 311, 312, 320, 339, 391, 435, 473, 474, 553, 568, 810, 824, 869, 893, 904 & 965

Stitches and Braids: Cloth stitch

Note: Colour change over shell.

SECTIONS 34 & 34A

Colours: 18, 218, 309, 339, 707 & 904

Stitches and Braids: Cloth stitch

SECTIONS 35 & 35A

Colours: < 35 > 5, 50, 215, 320, 473, 802 & 893

< 35a > add 454

Stitches and Braids: Cloth stitch

SECTIONS 36 & 36A

Colours: 130, 215, 320, 423, 454, 473, 474, 696, 802 & 893

Stitches and Braids: Cloth stitch

Note: Roll back.

SECTION 37

Colours: 3, 18, 283, 309, 336, 339, 483, 580, 582, 585, 835, 841, 869, 870 & 904

Stitches and Braids: Cloth stitch

Ribbon

Work the rolled, closed scroll thus:
Follow the notes given for working a closed scroll, Sea Swirl, section 63
Add extra prs to make the roll at the start #, work around the scroll
Before reaching the point where top sewings are to be made to join the scroll at its centre, the roll must first be worked far enough around the top of the scroll to enable the sewings to be made over the roll, pin A
(see 2.101)
Work continues with the braid, followed by the roll, pin B
If a roll is also to be made under the scroll on the other side of the braid, extra pairs can be added at the start and carried as inner passives, or they can be added when the sewings have been made and an edge pr is added, at pin X. In this way, the colours for the roll can be controlled (see 2.101)
This section is basically the same as Afterthoughts, sections 1 & 1a.
However, here it is worked differently, the working of the leaf towards the finish having been changed

SECTION 38

Colours: 18, 283, 309, 339, 582, 585 & 841

Stitches and Braids: Cloth stitch

Note: See section 37.

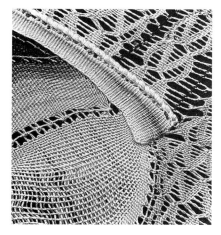

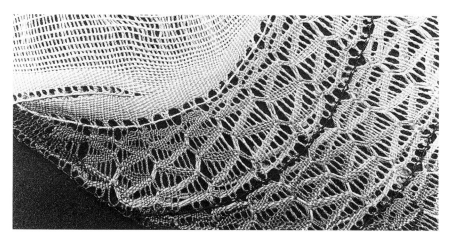

On Reflection (detail). Tenstick edge of shell, rolled back

On Reflection (detail). Joining the cloth st core of the shell with its textured exterior worked with Lotus 1

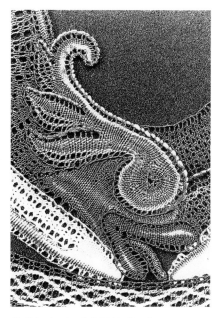

On Reflection: head of dolphin (detail)

SECTION 39
Colours: 18, 283, 309, 339, 582, 585, 835 & 841
Stitches and Braids: Cloth stitch

SECTION 40
Colours: 18, 309, 339, 582, 585 & 841
Stitches and Braids: Cloth stitch

SECTIONS 41 & 41A
Colours: 5, 50, 130, 215, 320, 339, 423, 454, 473, 474, 696, 802 & 893
Stitches and Braids: Cloth stitch & twist
Lotus 1

SECTIONS 42 & 42A
Colours: 5, 50, 130, 215, 320, 339, 423, 454, 473, 474, 696, 802 & 893
Stitches and Braids: Cloth stitch & twist
Lotus 1

SECTIONS 43 & 43A
Colours: 5, 50, 130, 215, 320, 339, 423, 454, 473, 474, 696, 802 & 893
Stitches and Braids: Cloth stitch & twist
Lotus 1

SECTIONS 44 & 44A
Colours: < 44 > 130, 215, 320, 339, 423, 473, 474, 696 & 893
< 44a > add 454
Stitches and Braids: Cloth stitch & twist

SECTIONS 45 & 45A
Colours: 130, 215, 320, 339, 423, 473, 474, 696 & 893
Stitches and Braids: Cloth stitch & twist
Lotus 1

Note: Side sewings into sections 44 & 44a.

SECTIONS 46 & 46A
Colours: 5, 130, 215, 320, 339, 423, 473, 474, 696, 802 & 893
Stitches and Braids: Cloth stitch & twist
Lotus 1

SECTIONS 47 & 47A
Colours: 130, 320, 339, 423, 473, 474, 696 & 893
Stitches and Braids: Cloth stitch & twist
Lotus 1 (var)

Note: See Sea Swirl, section 34, for Lotus 1, variation.

SECTIONS 48 & 48A
Colours: 130, 339, 423, 454, 473, 474 & 696

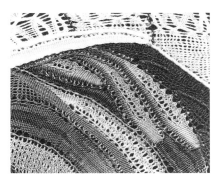

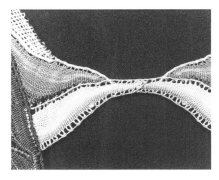

On Reflection: small fish, dolphin fins, fishtails and water (detail)

On Reflection (detail). Central joining of shells

Lotus 1 (var)

Note: See note section 47.

SECTIONS 51 & 51A
Colours: 130, 423, 474 & 696
Stitches and Braids: Cloth stitch & twist
Lotus 1 (var)

Note: Side sewings into sections 50 & 50a. See note section 47.

SECTIONS 52 & 52A
Colours: 423, 454, 473 & 696
Stitches and Braids: Cloth stitch & twist
Lotus 1 (var)

Note: See note section 47.

SECTIONS 53 & 53A
Colours: 130, 339 & 696
Stitches and Braids: Cloth stitch & twist

SECTION 54 & 54A
Colours: < 54 > 130, 339, 423 & 696
< 54a > omit 130
Stitches and Braids: Cloth stitch & twist

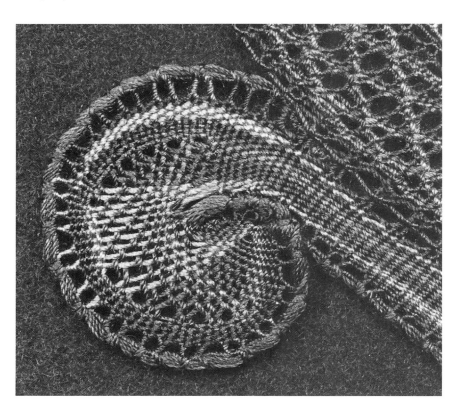

On Reflection (detail). Rolled scroll

Stitches and Braids: Cloth stitch & twist
Lotus 1 (var)

Note: Side sewings into sections 47 & 47a. See note section 47.

SECTIONS 49 & 49A
Colours: < 49 > 5, 130, 215, 320, 339, 423, 454, 473, 474 & 696
< 49a > omit 5

Stitches and Braids: Cloth stitch & twist
Lotus 1 (var)

Note: See note section 47.

SECTIONS 50 & 50A
Colours: 130, 339, 423, 454, 473, 474 & 696
Stitches and Braids: Cloth stitch & twist

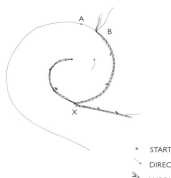

START
DIRECTION OF WORK
WORKING DIRECTION OF ROLL

2.101 On Reflection, working a rolled scroll in colour

On Reflection (detail). Shadows on fish, rolled closed scroll and further rolled edges on seaweed

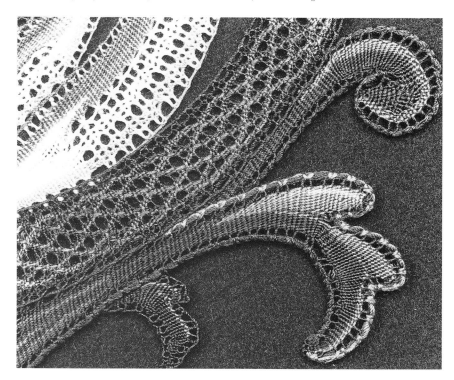

On Reflection (detail). Rolled scroll and leaf edge

EXPLAINING IDEAS

Chapter 3

This chapter explains a few of the ideas that have contributed to some previously published designs and offers a little more information on manipulating the threads to achieve painterly effects. The patterns and detailed information on working these designs can be found in *New Braids and Designs in Milanese Lace* by Patricia Read and Lucy Kincaid, published by B.T. Batsford Ltd. Also included in this chapter is the pattern for a privately commissioned piece, 'B' for Barry, which appears here with the kind permission of the owner.

GARLAND

Previously published in *New Braids and Designs in Milanese Lace*, Garland was inspired by the Venetian carousel in Paris, at the foot of the steps leading to Sacré-Coeur in Montmartre.

The carousel was decorated in the rococo style and was delicately ornate. Gilt scrolling and embellishments, often pastoral, surrounded scenes painted in soft, muted tones. When the carousel turned, the movement created by the delicate rococo designs

was further enhanced.

The movement of the carousel and its decoration are echoed by the constant twisting and turning of the leaves in Garland. An overall impression of the colours of the carousel comes with the addition of the two flower buds which, along with the leaves, are worked in soft, muted tones.

Sections 1, 2 & 3 of Garland show the leaves worked using the same techniques as those used for working the centre edge and controlled hole in sections 4a & 4b of Morning Glory (see 3.1).

The colours of the Garland flower bud, sections 5 & 6, are carefully blended, as in the petal sections, 4, 4a & 4b, of the Afternoon Dainties. Note the use of the lighter colour in section 7 where the braid, Lattice 3, is used as a filling.

The three main central shapes formed by the Garland and left open are an important feature of this design. However, with a careful choice of both texture and colour, they could be filled with fabric centres.

3.1 Garland, working direction of complex leaf form

MEDIEVAL PEACOCK

Previously published in *New Braids and Designs in Milanese Lace*, a simple two-tone design on an encaustic tile dating from the Middle Ages (see 3.2) provides the basic idea for the Medieval Peacock. The peacock's body at the centre of the tile changes into foliage as the design spirals out.

It is this metamorphosis that provides the key to this design. The vibrant colours of the peacock's feathers are used in an unrealistic way,

3.2 Medieval Peacock, medieval encaustic tile, original design

whilst still maintaining the essence of the subject. The areas of the design closest to the bird's body are dominated by purples, blues and turquoise. As the spiral opens out, and the leaf shapes occur, the foliage would be affected by sunlight. When this happens, the most dominant colours become blue/greens, dark greens and light acidic greens. These greens are also to be found on a peacock's feathers.

The use made of the light source is emphasized by the spiral having two sides, dark and light, similar in some respects to Celtic art. This design device also facilitates the working.

In section 9, the split in the braid can be achieved in the same way as in Fishtails (see 2.41). The leaf in section 9 is worked in the same way as the leaves in Garland (see 3.1), the instructions generally being the same as those given for working the centre edge and controlled hole of the flower, sections 4a & 4b, Morning Glory. The leaf buds, sections 9 & 10, are also worked with a controlled hole.

The braids were chosen to reflect the 'eye' shapes occurring on the tail feathers of a peacock. These braid shapes are used in a purely decorative

and non-representational way. In some cases only small sections, or pattern repeats, of the braids are used.

The glistening or metallic effect of the feathers was achieved by allowing the passive threads to be of local colour, i.e. the bird's neck and upper body is turquoise, blue and purple, and the leaders are of a contrasting colour, in this case golden yellow. When the work is viewed from different angles, the light appears to be reflecting off the bird's neck in different places. This is the result of the leaders showing through the tiny gaps left by the passive threads in cloth stitch. It is important not to allow the passives to be too closely packed together where the effect is to be most prominent. In this way the effect can be controlled (see 3.3 & 3.4).

GOLDEN YELLOW LEADERS

TURQ. BLUE + PURPLE PASSIVES

GOLDEN YELLOW LEADERS

TURQ. BLUE + PURPLE PASSIVES

3.3 & 3.4 Medieval Peacock, controlling the area of the effect caused when working with contrasting threads

The use of metallic threads is rarely successful in conveying the sense of shine, since the threads indiscriminately glitter and usually serve only to flatten the section they set out to describe. A shiny surface is one whose properties are areas of a highly contrasting nature, and so it is usually more effective to describe those different shapes individually. See the highlights on the wet seaweed, sections 10, 56, 57, 59, 60 & 61, of Sea Swirl.

'S' FOR SERPENT

This design won the Batsford Prize at the John Bull Trophy Exhibition 1993 and is previously published in *New Braids and Designs in Milanese Lace*.

In its original form, the initial 'S', weaving around a figure, was from a fifteenth-century choir book, though now detached, and probably illustrated St. Augustine. It is attributed to Belbello of Pavia, who was working in Milan during the early part of the fifteenth century and the style of whose work provides links with that of the sculptors working on Milan Cathedral during the same period.

As much Milanese lace was used for church vestments and altar cloths in the past, it seems quite fitting to use the basic form of this initial for a design in Milanese lace.

The only parts of the original initial to be retained are the basic shape and the central decoration. Serpents' heads, leaves akin to carnivorous plants and scrolls, replace stylized shells.

The colours in this piece are totally unrelated to the original. Instead, they depict serpents writhing amongst

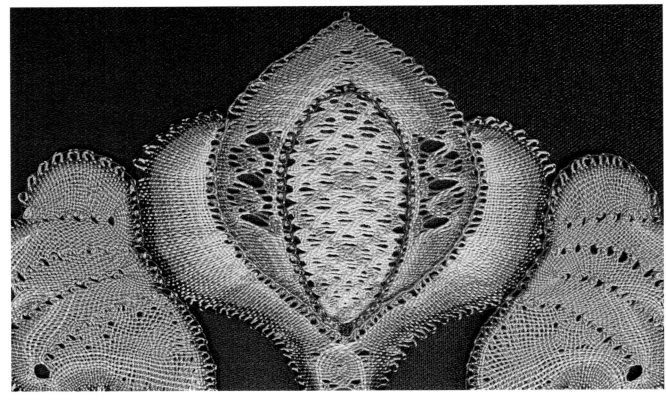

Garland (detail). Colour blending in flower and leaves. Fil à Dentelle (cotton)

foliage. The creams and greens of the leaves, and the creams, golds and turquoises of the scrolls, form an abstract pattern of diagonals which link the colours across the design.

Compositionally, the scrolls balance the design and give it a stability which contrasts with the movement of the serpents. The basic 'S' form of purples and blues is edged with creams and golds to link one corner of the diagonal with the other in opposition to the scrolls.

The pattern on the body of the lower serpent consists of colours which repeat at the wider sections of

Medieval Peacock (detail). Colour changes and effects on head and body when working with contrasting leaders. Gutermann Silk S 303

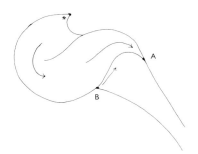

3.5 'S' for Serpent, changing the position of leaders, when working a complex leaf form

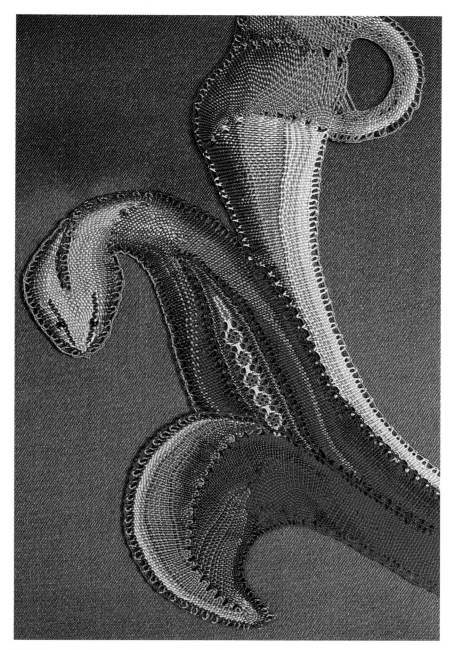

'S' for Serpent (detail). Effect of light on serpent's head and leaves. Gutermann Silk S 303

In section 13, the braid is split to work the top of the serpent's head, having added a pair to be leaders and a central edge pair as shown in Fishtails (see 2.28). Further along the serpent's body in the same section, the braid is split again; this time two central edge pairs and a leader pair are added, as shown in Fishtails (see 2.41).

The eyes of the serpents are created by the addition of very tiny beads, as follows. Thread a bead on to a fine crochet hook or doubled piece of wire. With the hook, pull one thread from the pair of bobbins through the bead to make a loop. Thread the other bobbin through the loop as if making a sewing. Tension both bobbins gently to ease the bead into position.

The appropriate use of beads in lace must be carefully considered. In this design, the eyes of the serpents, with their mesmerizing effect, play an important part. Due to the scale of the piece, if the eyes had been worked as small holes, they would have been barely noticeable. If the beads had been larger, they would then have dominated the piece, but for a different reason. Attention would be drawn to them primarily for being beads contrasting with the lace, rather than merely the serpents' eyes.

Shell and Seaweed Fan (detail). Colours in seaweed and worked shadows, also colour changes along edge of shell. Gutermann Silk S 303 (see also picture on page 126)

the initial. This is to indicate that the 'S' has also become a serpent's body that has twisted completely around itself.

The leaves have a similar working construction to those in Garland (see 3.1) and sections 4a & 4b, flower, Morning Glory. The main difference is that when, in sections 8, 9 & 11,

the leaders have worked the controlled hole and second side of the leaf, the leaders are tied off and thrown back at the edge, pin A. A new pair of leaders is added at the opposite edge, pin B, and worked across the pairs discarded at the edge pins of the second side of the leaf (see 3.5).

SHELL AND SEAWEED FAN

This design was the winner of the Nancy Armstrong Lace Fan Award and the Ian Ferris 3-D Trophy at the John Bull Trophy Exhibition 1993, and can be found in the previously published *New Braids and Designs in Milanese Lace*.

Fascination with the illusory effects that can be achieved when colour is carefully used, plus a scallop shell, inspired this design. The dark and richly coloured seaweed contrasts with the pale and delicately coloured shell, and a strong graphic image is produced. By introducing shadows, worked into the braids of the shell, a three-dimensional trompe-l'oeil effect is created which strengthens the image further.

To achieve this effect, part of the seaweed is worked away from the edge of the shell. On completion of the design, this part of the seaweed is twisted and attached to the side of the shell. It is allowed to hang in a position where it creates its own shadow next to the seaweed with the worked shadows. If the light source is correctly placed, the difference between the real and fake shadows disappears.

Part of the success of this effect depends upon using a colour range with even tonal differences, so that each thread colour can be given the same tonal value when depicting the area of shadow. It is worth remembering that when a shadow is cast, there is usually a colour change in addition to a tonal change, caused by reflected colour influences and the colour of the light. For the Shell and Seaweed Fan, the light source was imagined to be bright daylight casting a blue bias into the shadows.

To emphasize the effect of the light source even further, the undulating edge of the shell was exaggerated and drawn with a scalloped edge. When the Tenstick edge was worked, the scallops which were to be in shadow were worked with darker, bluer threads. Richness and depth of colour in the seaweed is due in part to the tonal equality of the dark green and use of its dark red complementary colour.

The positioning of the dark red threads could have caused problems when working the free section of seaweed, since it would not be desirable to throw back threads which would be visible on completion. If the red threads had remained continually in the same position, the seaweed would probably have resembled a striped ribbon. By manipulating the threads so that they all moved in a particular sequence, the appearance of error was eliminated and the red threads formed their own descriptive pattern. In the same way, the different tones of green could be moved around, so that the seaweed appeared to be more natural.

The threads were manipulated in a similar way as in the lattice braids, but without twisting the leaders, so that the seaweed remained flat and closely worked. Extra threads were added to widen the braid, and by their positioning they enabled the thread movements to be even more varied.

The wooden fan-sticks made from holly by John Brooker were specially commissioned to fit the fan leaf.

'B' FOR BARRY

When designing a commissioned piece of work, especially an initial, creating a design that has a personal relevance becomes a major consideration. This piece of work was commissioned by a maker of exquisite bobbins. In the following notes some of the design considerations will be explained, though not all the personal references.

Falling into the trap of producing a design with a wholly pictorial theme would be all too easy, and over a period of time most probably assume no more relevance than a child's alphabet. Equally there is a need for certain personal points of reference, otherwise the reason and desire to commission the piece of work no longer exists. It is hoped, then, that a balance is to be struck between producing a design that in itself is satisfying and worthwhile, whilst also being meaningful to the owner.

The font style chosen for this design is the one used by the owner already and known as Baghdad. Obviously, many alterations have been made to the letter, but the base shape remains true. The Baghdad theme is continued with the choice of braids, inspired by the architecture and decoration found in the Middle East.

The colours chosen relate very closely to those used by the bobbin maker on his bobbins, and the essence of the decorative style he employs is echoed in the design lines.

Pricking Size: See 3.6 & 3.7
100%: Gutermann Silk S 303

Thread: Gutermann Silk S 303 is shown in the sample.

Colours: 5, 37, 43, 50, 130, 143, 158, 213, 214, 215, 218, 309, 311, 369, 384, 423, 454, 568, 658, 659, 696, 802 & 810

Stitches and Braids: Tenstick
Cloth stitch
Lattice 3
Maltese spot
Crossnet
Basketweave
Bubbles
Lattice 2
Lattice 1
Archway

'B' for Barry (detail). Upper loop, Maltese spots and colour changes in Tenstick

To Work: The threads used to produce the example are listed for guidance only. The execution of the design is entirely at the discretion of the lacemaker. Different threads and colours may be used, in which case the size of the pricking may need to be adjusted accordingly.

Before commencing work, make a second copy of the pricking and draw in the outlines of each section. If using different threads or colours, also make a colour study to refer to as work progresses.

Work each section numerically as shown in 3.6 & 3.7. See 3.6 & 3.7 for start # of each section and direction of work.

No (colour) change stitch is used throughout. Top sewings are used throughout. After sections 1, 2 & 3 have been worked, the ends of the threads are cut off and loosely plaited, leaving them long enough to rewind on to bobbins for eventual top sewing into section 13. They can be tucked out of the way while the other sections are worked. Do not sew the ends from sections 1, 2 & 3 into section 13 until after section 15 has been worked. Leave out pairs at each central pin, to be collected later, when reaching the acute angles in sections 3 & 10. Use magic threads where appropriate. Expect to change both the pattern passives and leaders throughout the working of this piece.

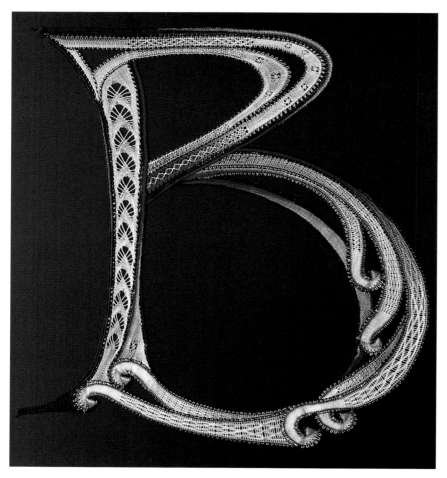

'B' for Barry. Gutermann Silk S 303

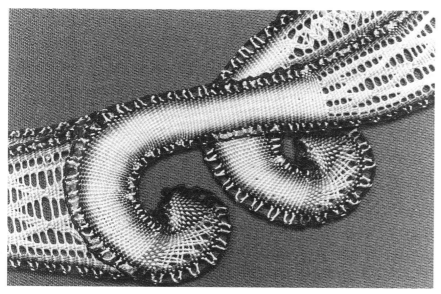

'B' for Barry (detail). Use of shaded colours in scrolls

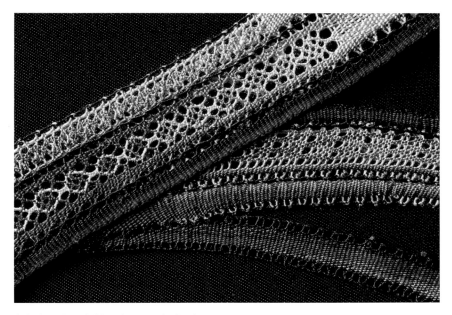

'B' for Barry (detail). Colour changes within braids

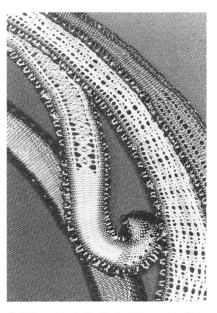

'B' for Barry (detail). Shading in cloth st and braids; Bubbles, Lattice 1 and 2

'B' for Barry (detail). Shading in Tenstick and braids; Archway, Crossnet and Bubbles

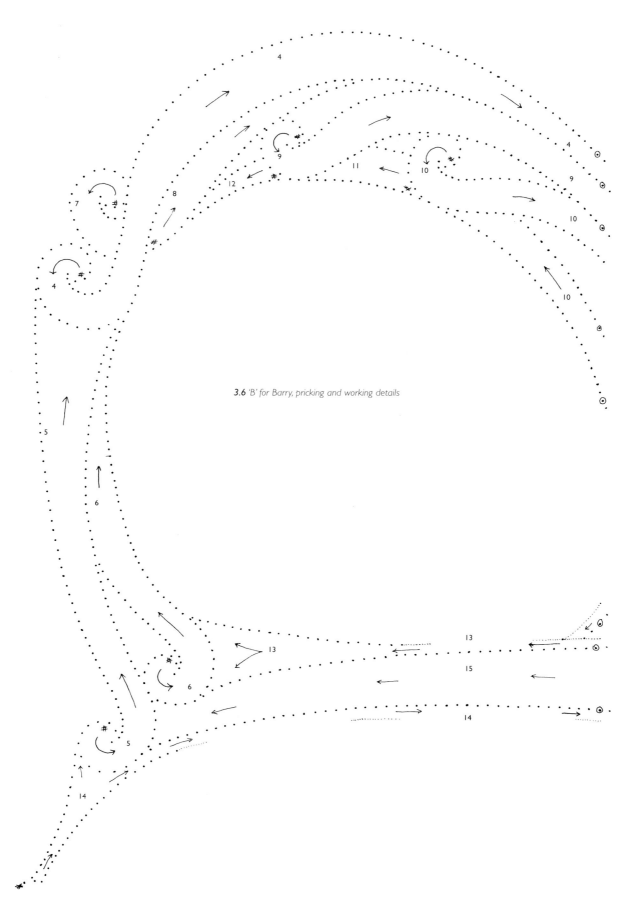

3.6 'B' for Barry, pricking and working details

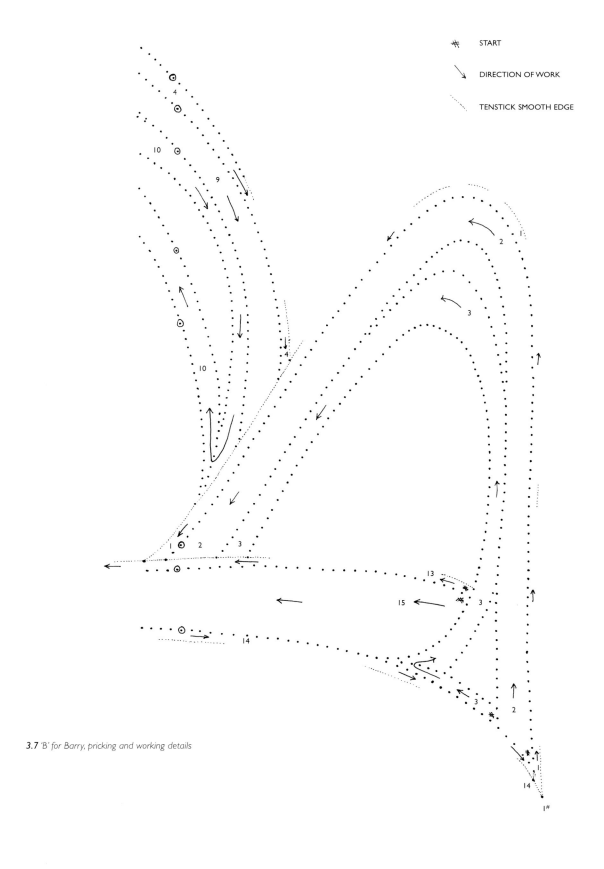

START

DIRECTION OF WORK

TENSTICK SMOOTH EDGE

3.7 'B' for Barry, pricking and working details

SUPPLIERS

THREADS

Barnyarns
c/o Madeira Threads (UK) Ltd
Thirsk Industrial Park
York Road
Thirsk
North Yorkshire YO7 3BX

Stitches and Lace
Alby Craft Centre
Cromer Road
Alby
Norfolk NR11 7QE

Tim Parker
124 Corhampton Road
Bournemouth
Dorset BH6 5NZ

Pipers Silks
Chinnerys
Egremont Street
Glemsford
Suffolk CO10 7RS

GENERAL SUPPLIERS

D.J. Hornsby
25 Manwood Avenue
Canterbury
Kent CT2 7AH

Spinneyhill Lacemaking Supplies
144 Bush Road
Cuxton
Rochester
Kent ME2 1HB

FURTHER READING

Patricia Read and Lucy Kincaid, *Milanese Lace*, B.T. Batsford Ltd, London, 1988.

Patricia Read and Lucy Kincaid, *New Braids and Designs in Milanese Lace*, B.T. Batsford Ltd, 1994.

Trude v.d. Heijden-Biemans, Yvonne Scheele-Kerkhof and Puck Smelter-Hoekstra, *Withof Lace*, B.T. Batsford Ltd, 1991.

Christine and David Springett, *The Torchon Lace Book*, Christine and David Springett, 1993.

ndex